The Lost Road Home

Jimmy

Best of Luck to you always!

God Bless You...

Milly

The Lost Road Home

Post Traumatic Stress Disorder (PTSD)
And the Psychological Effects of War
On Veterans and Their Families

By Milly Balzarini

DeForest Press
Rogers, Minnesota

Permission gratefully acknowledged to Dr. Dan Forrester and Robin Kennedy for use of materials previously published in their dissertations, to Ed Walters for his painting used as background for the cover, and for use of poems written by Noah Charles Pierce (copyright 2007 Cheryl Softich).

Published by:
DeForest Press
P.O. Box 383
Rogers, MN 55374 United States
www.DeForestPress.com
Toll-free: 866-509-0604
Shane Groth, Publisher
Richard DeForest Erickson, Founder

Cover design by Linda Walters, Optima Graphics, Appleton, WI
Author photo by Kyle R. Miron, CK Unlimited Photography

ISBN 978-1-930374-27-0

Printed in the United States of America
11 10 09 08   5 4 3 2 1

Library of Congress Cataloging-in-Publication Data

Balzarini, Milly, 1948-
   The lost road home : post traumatic stress disorder (PTSD) and the psychological effects of war on veterans and their families / by Milly Balzarini.
      p. ; cm.
   Includes bibliographical references.
   ISBN 978-1-930374-27-0
   1. Post-traumatic stress disorder. 2. Post-traumatic stress disorder--Patients--Family relationships. 3. Veterans--Mental health. I. Title. II. Title: Post traumatic stress disorder (PTSD) and the psychological effects of war on veterans and their families.
   [DNLM: 1. Stress Disorders, Post-Traumatic--United States--Personal Narratives. 2. Combat Disorders--psychology--United States--Personal Narratives. 3. Family Relations--United States--Personal Narratives. 4. Social Support--United States--Personal Narratives. 5. Veterans--psychology--United States--Personal Narratives. WM 170 B198L 2008]
   RC552.P67B328 2008
   616.85'212--dc22
                              2008004695

Dedicated
to
All Veterans

and

In memory of

Chris Hoyum and Noah Pierce

Chris Hoyum

Noah Pierce

Contents

Foreword

Like waves on ruffled water, driven by the wind to a fate, not of their own making, but by the power they entrusted, they rose up to meet the wind and were carried to whatever destiny awaited them. Relentlessly enduring until spent by the experience, used up by the power that spurred them on, they finally dissipated on the shore of the home they had left.

This is the story of American soldiers caught in a wind created by their government who said it would stop the spread of Communism by sending waves of men to Vietnam to endure the storm. After fighting, the soldiers found themselves back on the shores of their country with people who were unappreciative, gave them no recognition, and who did not care to understand what they had endured.

The war was long and the enemy elusive. It was a political war with directives from above affecting the way the war was fought and the eventual outcome.

There were many heroes, soldiers who put their lives on the line for others. There were countless acts of heroism. The conditions that they fought in were often unbearable. The circumstances during which they served their country were the worst and they are yet to be welcomed home. Many of these soldiers have continued to carry tremendous burdens—the after effects of their experiences. The quality of their lives was greatly changed.

This is a book about war, about the veterans and their families. It is both a way to honor veterans and to genuinely understand the sacrifice they and their families have made because they served their country.

The author knows of what she speaks. She is the wife of a Vietnam veteran. She has lived the aftermath of the war as it affected her husband and consequently her family. He was a great warrior who has ever so gradually been readjusting to being home. She has kept the family together and functioning while at the same time coping with the burden that her husband still carries. She may be responsible for keeping him alive when he went through his darkest moments. Many Vietnam veterans succumbed to the allure of suicide, finally able to put the war behind them. Estimates are that 350,000 have committed suicide. Fourteen thousand more die each year as the result of suicide and accidental deaths. If they would have been told that they would experience readjustment problems and that there was help available it may have saved many lives.

At the time this book is being written the Afghanistan and Iraq wars continue. Veterans of these wars are being informed of possible readjustment problems. They are also being welcomed home as heroes. The Vietnam veterans paved the way for these veterans to never have to experience not knowing what is wrong with them and the American public is not taking their dissatisfaction with the war out on the American soldier. Hopefully they can also take satisfaction out of having survived the most difficult of circumstances. They are heroes every one of them.

As for those who did not return and gave the ultimate sacrifice, the surviving Vietnam veterans can honor them by going on with their lives, finding purpose and living life as full and meaningful as possible. This may mean simply getting well and taking care of their families and helping others, perhaps new veterans.

As you read this book, you will gain a greater understanding of what these courageous soldiers have endured and honor them for the sacrifice they have made.

Dan Forrester Ph.D., LMSW
Veterans Adjustment Counselor

Preface

My main purpose in writing this book is to create an awareness of post-traumatic stress disorder (PTSD) so the families of Iraq veterans can recognize the symptoms and take the first steps towards healing. I hope they do not have to live and suffer with PTSD, undiagnosed, for years as many Vietnam veterans have.

This book includes true accounts of what veterans experienced during war. These interviews often come word for word from the veterans themselves. The names have been changed but the accounts of their experiences are true. Soldiers are trained and conditioned to fight and to kill…and then they are expected to forget it all and come back to civilian life unscathed. While many of the veterans I interviewed fought in Vietnam, others fought in Iraq, Korea and World War II. I've included examples of the trauma they have endured and how it affected their postwar lives years later, along with the effect it has had on their families. It is not a pretty picture, but there are signs of hope as both veterans and others learn and appreciate the far-reaching effects of PTSD.

One of my goals is to help create an attitude in our society of compassion for these soldiers and to instill a minimum level of patriotism, social conscience, and tolerance—to accept these "damaged goods," so to speak. Post-traumatic stress disorder is not an excuse for bad behavior, but it is an explanation for the way people behave and why they react the way they do. Rather than making these soldiers castaways, my hope is that employers, families and society in general will recognize the problem and provide help, appreciating the unselfish sacrifice these soldiers have made for them as fellow citizens of the United States.

My thanks and sincere gratitude go out to the veterans who have freely shared their stories and feelings, even though many of their experiences were painful to relive. You are my heroes.

To Dan Forrester, Ph.D., who has been a godsend to many veterans. He has been guiding these veterans along their difficult journey, counseling them and leading them to a healing place. He has encouraged me to write and his encouragement and support made me believe that I could. Thanks also to Dan for allowing me to use portions of his dissertation, which contained a wealth of valuable information.

To Gary Klar, Ph.D., Utah State, a Vietnam veteran, and to Anthony Leonhart (B.S., Iowa State University), for proofreading and giving me some assistance in editing along the way.

To Robin J. Kennedy for allowing me to use some of her wonderful research and information contained in her master's thesis.

To my wonderful family…to my husband who freely shared his feelings, experiences, and his journal with me and did not think about his own regard, but truly and sincerely wanted to help other veterans, particularly those coming home from Iraq. And to my daughters who allowed me to share our lives with the world. No one could have kids as wonderful as you.

I want to sincerely thank the publishers, Shane Groth and Dick Erickson, for their hard work and support. Shane is a talented, intelligent professional who has worked diligently to edit and shape this book. He has brought it from a rough draft to a polished piece of work.

Dick and Shane shared my enthusiasm and belief that this was a story and topic that needed to be told. The passion we all felt about this book and the men who told these stories created a bond between us. They have made this mission of mine to write this book a reality, a dream come true.

Post-Traumatic Stress Disorder in the Balzarini Home

"Another guy and I were carrying a wounded soldier on a stretcher. I felt the back of the stretcher drop, and I looked back. The guy who had been holding up the other end didn't have a head."

Steve, a Vietnam veteran

What's Happened to My World?

It was a quiet Saturday afternoon when I first learned about PTSD. I was getting caught up on chores around the house and was folding laundry in the living room and watching TV at the same time. I happened to be watching the PBS channel which was being broadcast from our local university television station. A program featuring Vietnam veterans and a counselor was on. The veterans were relating some of their reactions, feelings and behaviors since they had returned from Vietnam 30 or more years ago. They were speaking of anger, the outbursts, the depression, and their inability to cope with life in general. Words such as impatience, hypervigilance, and stress were common as each Vietnam veteran told his story.

I put down the towel I was folding and began to listen more attentively. I could relate to everything they said! They were describing my husband! I had missed the first portion of the program but the last 20 minutes had my undivided attention.

At the end of the program the counselor listed two telephone numbers in case anyone was interested in more information. I quickly grabbed a scrap of paper and a pen and wrote down the numbers. I needed to find out more about this PTSD. When the moment was right I would tell Ted about what I had learned. I would tell him I thought I finally knew what was wrong…

I always knew there was something wrong. I wasn't sure what it was, but I knew that something wasn't right. I remember sitting in church with Ted and fighting back tears. I was praying that God would help my husband. I was praying that God would help me to cope. I had attended this church with him many times, and we had been married here. We had stood at this altar and recited our wedding vows 34 years ago. In sickness and in health, for richer, for poorer, until death do we part. I tried to swallow that huge lump in my throat and tried to conceal my emotion, but many times as we sang "Let There be Peace on Earth and Let It Begin With Me" it triggered deep emotions within me. I wondered how long I could stay in a marriage like this. It was so confusing. At times I was so happy, and I knew that Ted loved me and our children, but then there were the outbursts of anger, that short fuse, the constant underlying anger and negativity that we all dealt with. The unpredictable behaviors which caused us to all walk on eggs. He was like a time bomb, and we never knew when he would explode.

So many questions went through my mind over the years when I would witness this behavior. Ted's mother had been mentally ill for many years and had lived in and out of institutions for most of our marriage. Each time she was given a chance to live in her own home it would result in a suicide attempt. The thought of mental illness was in the back of my mind. But Ted was so intelligent, and most of the time he was fine. Was it a dysfunctional home that he was brought up in? Or was he just a spoiled brat? So many things went through my mind. What made people act the way that they did? What could explain this behavior? Where do I begin?

Ted was born on August 16, 1947, a beautiful healthy baby boy. Shortly after his birth, his mother suffered from a very severe post partum depression. In 1947 there were no anti-depressants, no Prozac or Paxil, no explanation to what was happening to his mother. She lay in bed day after day at the homestead of her in-laws unable to take care of her newborn son. Her depression had been so debilitating that she was incapable of doing anything to care for Ted. She barely looked at him. And so for the first few years of his life his grandma and Uncle Donald nurtured him and loved him. Eventually his mother, after many months, began to recuperate from her depression and in time Ted and his mother and father left the grandparents' home to live in a home of their own. This was extremely difficult for his grandmother who had grown to love him like her own.

At times their life was dysfunctional, like many families, but for the most part Ted was happy. He attended a parochial school and later graduated from the public school system.

Ted and I met while he was a senior in high school while riding on the same school bus. I was spending the night at a friend's house and she always sat with him on the bus. I didn't pay too much attention to him at the time but later in the week I ran into him in the halls in school. He was always friendly and smiled at me. He had brown hair and brown eyes and was tall and nice looking.

One night I was attending the Saturday night school dance when he suddenly came over to talk to me. Our conversation was interesting and we spent the rest of the evening together talking and listening to the '60s tunes that were playing in the background. Before the night was over he had invited me to go to our favorite local hangout for a pizza. That was the beginning of our high school romance.

We spent a lot of time together going to movies, bowling, swimming, and just laughing and talking. In 1966 we were both attending the local university, Northern Michigan University (NMU). Neither of us were serious students and although we did attend a lot of classes, we frequently cut classes to sit and drink coffee in the cafeteria. Ted also spent a lot of time playing pool or cards with his friends. We were pretty immature and our lack of dedication to our classes was reflected in our grades.

In the middle of Ted's sophomore year at NMU he and his best friend decided that since they would probably be drafted into the army eventually, they would volunteer for the draft. When he broke the news to his parents they were very upset. Most young men were being sent to Vietnam who had volunteered and they didn't want to see him in danger.

Ted did his basic training at Fort Campbell, Kentucky. Then he went to Fort Polk, Louisiana, for Advanced Infantry Training (AIT) at Tigerland, where he trained hard. At Fort Campbell, Kentucky, he and two others had an MOS (military occupational specialty) of 11 Bravo, as this company was rated very high for physical training scores. Luck of the draw, it was a bad start. So it was on to Fort Polk, or Tigerland, as it was

Ted at Tigerland.

known to all who trained there. It was famous for guerrilla warfare training.

Ted and his two close AIT buddies would discuss further training opportunities. They wanted to stay together but chose differently regardless of it. Ted wanted to attend NCO (Non Commissioned Officer) School at Fort Benning, Georgia, first. The other two wanted to go to jump school, so that's where they parted. Ted had decided that the more training he could get, the better his chances were to survive this hitch. So after a twenty-day leave he returned to Fort Benning and was visited by one of the guys attending jump school, who told him that he and his whole class were going to Germany. Ted never saw, or heard from, this guy again.

At Fort Benning his training was intense and conducted by Army Rangers. This was 13 weeks of hell, and then it was on to Fort Polk again for some "on the job" training (OJT). Ted was the platoon sergeant for an AIT group going through Tigerland's training for another eight weeks. All of this training was setting the post-traumatic-stress-disorder train in motion.

He was given a leave after basic training and before he left for Vietnam. During this time at home we became engaged to be married. I had written to him almost every day and this Christmas was special. We had talked about our hopes and dreams a million times. We would get married and have babies and live happily ever after.

Ted left for Vietnam in January of 1969. He had trained so hard that he felt like he had trained for the Olympics. He felt like he was ready for Vietnam. He was in perfect physical condition, had grown up a lot and I thought he was more handsome than ever. I loved and respected him more than I ever did and it was heartbreaking to see him leave. His mother and father were worried sick about him. It would be a very long year.

Ted's Story

We flew into Vietnam at dusk. When I got off of the plane it was so hot. They put us on buses (almost like prison buses with mesh on the windows). Finally we got to the repo depo. There were burms and embankments, and there were barracks, but they were mostly occupied and we would have had to walk through and find a place to sleep. It was night and so I threw my duffle bag on the ground and slept on the street. So did a lot of other guys. It would be morning in just a few hours.

My first day in the bush in Vietnam, the squad I was to be leading was guarding water point. When I arrived I was told to go down to the river to introduce myself to the guys as their new squad leader. As I approached the stream I saw that they were playing with a huge python and her baby. I had always been deathly afraid of snakes, but I wasn't about to let them know it. I introduced myself and sat back on the bank and had a smoke. I didn't say a word about the snake and just let them have their fun. Eventually they let the snakes go. I had just gone through basic training, Advanced Infantry Training, Noncommissioned Officers School, and had trained for thirteen weeks with the Rangers. Here I was after all of that training, on my first day in the bush thinking, "Don't tell me it's going to be like this every day." It wasn't the first thing that I wanted to run into. I'd had lots of encounters, but Pythons weren't one of them. Snakes gave me the willies.

We lived a kind of primitive life. Our clothes used to practically rot off of us because of the sweat and the salt that would dry into our clothes. Any little stick or thorn would tear our clothes and after a while we barely had any clothes. They were in shreds. We used our helmets as a washbasin to wash our faces and shave. We didn't always have a toothbrush and so when we were near a pond we would wash up and brush our teeth with sand and our fingers. We weren't always resupplied with the things we needed. At times we were in extreme conditions. We were in dangerous areas where even the helicopters couldn't come in. Many times we went without food and water. We would look for wild cucumbers to eat. There were banana trees but the bananas didn't ripen enough to eat until days after they were picked.

I remember a helicopter coming in to resupply us in the boonies and to bring another replacement to our company. The helicopter was hovering 40 feet above us and I not only could see our replacement but I could smell the brand of soap he had used. We hadn't had a bath or a change of clothing in 40 days and so I can just imagine what we all smelled like to him.

The first time I was on patrol with my company I was sent to Ban me Tuit. That particular terrain is heavy underbrush cover and the easiest trails to follow were made by the largest animals such as elephants or water buffalo. As a new sergeant, my CO (commanding officer) decided to have me take (walk) point. The point man has the compass and leads the whole column. I was a new guy and he was going to test me. As I broke my way through heavy underbrush I noticed a well-worn elephant trail which was pretty much paralleling my route, so rather than fight the heavy brush I decided to follow this trail. Upon coming to the end of this trail I stopped and was baffled because the trail ended and I saw no elephant. All of a sudden two or three elephants got up from wherever they were lying down and made that loud shrill shriek they make when they are scared or charging. All of a sudden there was brush breaking and elephants running. My heart almost stopped. I was so startled that I hit the deck, taking a position of defense. The CO called forward from his radio and asked, "What the hell's going on up there?!" I responded that we surprised some elephants and they ran off screaming. The CO asked if they were humpin' anything. I asked, "What do you mean?" He said, "I mean were they carrying anything?" (The North Vietnamese

Ted setting up a night ambush.

used animals to carry weapons and supplies.) I said I was too startled to notice.

You must look and listen for the desperation of seeking safety, brought on by the fear of escaping impending death. The vastness of distance to safety is a world away. With each step, with each glance, with each breath one takes, your senses are heightened, and then deflated, and then rapidly brought back to maximum sensitivity. This repeated exercise is the Combat Infantry Search and Destroy Mission response to dangerous surroundings, always planning for the worst should it happen right now. The visible enemy is watching my approach and I must react to minimize his effect on me and my comrades. This is on my mind night and day.

The combat infantryman is always sharpening his keen senses because this is what is relied on to get us through. I am expected to perform, to protect myself. Others rely on me for their safety. My men would ask me if I was scared. I would reply that I wasn't the most scared over here, but I would bet it was in the top ten! They would laugh, but they knew it was good to be afraid because it made you alert and sensitive to every encounter, and it caused you to assess the situations. It made for very good jungle bunnies. Stealth is practiced to peak performances and it yielded fewer casualties. It also helps self confidence to take control. This means, "I can do it better, and I trust me over you." We therefore reluctantly gave up control and took it back the first chance we got.

The Central Highlands have double and triple canopy forests with some small openings but not big enough to get a chopper in. I remember this well for many reasons. One very hot day we were climbing one of these wooded mountains, on which I had followed a well-worn tiger trail. We stopped briefly to rest. We were close to our day's destination and we moved up to the top. My squad had the point. Two men were ahead of me. We moved about three to five meters apart, and when we reached the top, several shots from an AK-47 on my right popped, and then a few more. I had returned fire and had deployed the remainder of the squad to allow me to go forward as I had two men down. One man was shot through the abdomen, so I moved to the other man who was lying on his back with his rifle lying across his neck. I removed his weapon and saw that there was a bullet hole in his throat. He whispered to me, "Am I hit bad?" I replied, "Hell no, you're not even bleeding." I am sure the bleeding was internal and the bullet was lodged in his spine. He could still talk and move his eyes. I was afraid that he was going into shock. We had to get him out so we used bars of C-4 (an explosive) to blow a couple of large trees out so a chopper could get in for the pick up.

We secured the area and dug foxholes about two to three feet deep and formed a circular perimeter. As night fell we fell asleep. I was totally physically and mentally exhausted. We were mortared that night and were attacked by ground troops. Our guys didn't fire too many shots but instead threw grenades at the sound of movement. As the mortars were coming in I was sleeping on the ground. I could hear the bursts, but I was too tired to wake up. My CO (company commander) hollered, "Balzarini, get in your hole!" I reluctantly obeyed, went in the hole, and fell back to sleep.

After a little rest, morning light appeared so I got up to participate in the ritual morning stand. We brought our outposts in as we had to move out. Ten feet from my knee-deep hole was an NVA (North Vietnamese Army) helmet with one star. I was told it was the rank of lieutenant. Somebody got close to me that night the CO told me. He then said, "Balzarini, get us out of here! Take point." Glover and I shared a two-man point 30 meters apart. It took us an hour to move the company 500 meters. We set up camp again early hoping we were being watched. As soon as night fell we silently moved to the next hill. It had been held for us by another squad sent there earlier that day. We sat up that evening in a wait and see, to see if our earlier position would be hit. It was, and the forward observer officer had the game set for artillery to hit that place hard once the shit hit the fan. Not only could we see the position being hit, but we could see where it was coming from so we ripped them a new ass with artillery all night.

We were told we would be air lifted by helicopter to a hot landing zone (LZ)—place where we would be fired upon by the enemy as soon as we landed. It would be very dangerous and we were actually given the Last Rights before we boarded the helicopter. As we got off we had to protect ourselves with our rucksacks and be ready to head for cover. I didn't expect to survive this and kept thinking it could be the last moments of my life. As it turned out, the enemy had left the area.

This is one of the times where we were ready for the worst. It seemed to take forever for the anxiety to settle after knowing we were in a relatively safe LZ. However, there are times when we experienced the opposite, where we thought the supposed area we were landing in was safe enough to regroup and to move on for further deployment, only to find yourself being fired at as you approached. You know that everybody is going to be somewhat panicky about being surprised even though you anticipate such an occurrence. Squad leaders, platoon sergeants are shouting commands to regroup to minimize time and casualties and to re-deploy either defensively or an offensive assault. You just never know.

During the dry season we were out of water. We were down to our last swallow and some guys didn't even have that. We came along a dry creek bed where there was some smoldering debris from previous shelling. We gathered in platoon groups and sent a few men from each group with a shovel to go and dig in the dry creek bed to see if there might be some water. It was a desperate hope to find some moisture. While we stood around complaining, half of us bare-skinned and taking a rest, the officers (company commander and lieutenants) gathered to make a call to battalion firebase and requested that they send a chopper out with water to resupply us, as we had nothing and could not move anywhere. The battalion commander's reply was, "I have no birds available, make do with what you have" (which was nothing).

About ten minutes later, while in a discussion with a platoon leader and others, I happened to notice movement through the corner of my eye about 100 meters out of the wood line. I grabbed my weapon and ran towards the person who just stood there and was not brandishing a weapon. All of a sudden he started running away. Within a few seconds I caught up to him and shouted, while discharging one round into the air. I marched him back to our CP (command post). He picked up his helmet and we found his weapon on the way, which had one star on it, meaning he was a lieutenant in the North Vietnamese Army.

Our company alerted the battalion commander that we had a prisoner. I was standing right there so I heard every word of his conversation. The battalion commander said he'd send a chopper out to pick him up. Including myself and several others, we said to the company commander, "You tell that S.O.B. that if there isn't any water on that f'n chopper, he's not getting his prisoner!" They cared more about the prisoner and the credit the battalion commander would get than they cared about us. I get mad about how we were treated over there and I think about how the Iraq soldiers are being treated.

As I think about getting that prisoner, I think about how stupid it was to run towards him because if there had been another NVA person in the woods I would have gotten shot. However, I took the chance and I'm glad I didn't have to shoot him. As I've thought about him years later, I wonder if he received humane treatment and if he ever thinks about how an American soldier spared his life.

I was in Bravo, 2nd of the 35th, 4th Infantry Division. We were in the mountains and had run out of supplies. It rained for three days and we were camped on a hill. The ground was wet, and the hills were greasy and slippery. It was muddy and wet and we had no food. I remembered that not far away we had come through an abandoned mountain yard village where I saw a small piece of corn and some cucumbers still growing. So I went back there and got them. My mother had sent me a package that had bouillon cubes in it and so that's pretty much all we had to eat. After three days we walked 16,000 meters back to the firebase after not eating. We were all tired and extremely hungry. The cans of food, which were meant for us, were sitting there, but before we could eat anything we got an ass chewing

After the dry season Ted traded in his "boonie hat" for a dry helmet.
Milly's name was written on the front and a crucifix was on the back of the helmet.
Ponchos (a shelter half) made a two-man pup tent.

from the battalion commander because he said we didn't do anything for three days. We didn't shoot anyone, we didn't have any prisoners, and no head count. It wasn't until we got chewed out that we were able to eat. The biggest man in the platoon, we called him "Tiny," wrote a letter to his congressman and told them about how we were treated.

Our battalion commander didn't last long. We never saw him again. I hope it was due to the letter to the congressman. The way we were treated and forgotten...no one gave a shit. The battalion commander cared more about looking good and a good body count than he cared about his own men. I think even our dogs were treated better than that.

It was March 7, 1969. We had another tough day. I was leading the company on point to a predetermined area to assist another company that had been pinned down and couldn't get to their dead and wounded. When we got to where we were going we started taking on small arms fire and we got pinned down as well. There was no decent cover to advance to. The lieutenant went forward with his radioman and the radioman got shot through the heart. The lieutenant and I felt bad that we weren't able to avoid this from happening. My company commander came up and he saw that the radio operator was shot and he looked at me and said, "Come on, Sarge! Let's get that son of a bitch!"

I grabbed a couple of guys and an RPG rocket exploded in front of us. We all took some shrapnel but we managed to fight for some time. I was trying to low crawl to another spot, and eventually I got to where I wanted to be. Up ahead I saw movement. One of our guys was hunched over in front of me and I didn't want to hit him. I told another guy up ahead of me that there was someone there and to throw a grenade at the enemy, but he didn't have a grenade so I threw him one. Just at that moment he got shot in the ass. That told me that the shot was coming from behind us. The grenade ended up hitting him in the head and he couldn't pick it up.

A guy next to me, one of ours, took one through the skull. He was dead. There was brush and trees all around and the enemy was hidden and seemed to be all around us. Not only was I getting fired at from enemy ahead of me and from the side, but also from behind me. I had to stop pursuing the enemy in front and redirect my fire to those who had gotten behind us and to our left flank. I had to get the guy that was shooting at us from behind our guy that was hunched over. I was shooting so close to him that I knocked the first aid kit off of his belt, but luckily I didn't hit him. I sprayed the hell out of the place and either got the guy or he ran away. I never did get the opportunity to check.

When they dragged the man out that was hunched over in

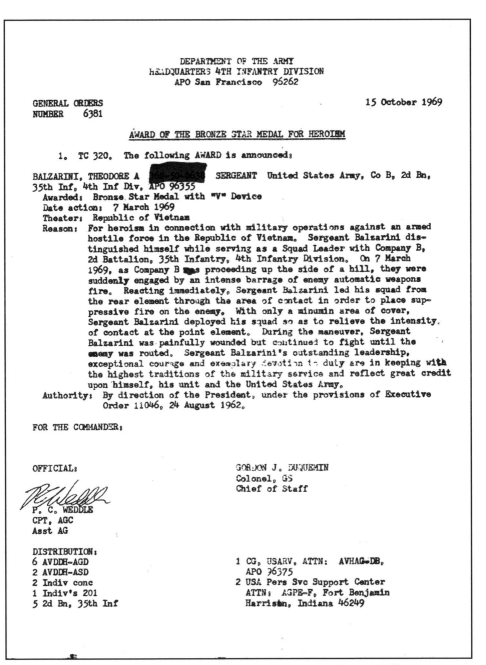

DEPARTMENT OF THE ARMY
HEADQUARTERS 4TH INFANTRY DIVISION
APO San Francisco 96262

GENERAL ORDERS　　　　　　　　　　　　　　　15 October 1969
NUMBER　6381

AWARD OF THE BRONZE STAR MEDAL FOR HEROISM

1. TC 320. The following AWARD is announced:

BALZARINI, THEODORE A ██████ SERGEANT United States Army, Co B, 2d Bn,
35th Inf, 4th Inf Div, APO 96355
　Awarded: Bronze Star Medal with "V" Device
　Date action: 7 March 1969
　Theater: Republic of Vietnam
　Reason: For heroism in connection with military operations against an armed
　　hostile force in the Republic of Vietnam. Sergeant Balzarini dis-
　　tinguished himself while serving as a Squad Leader with Company B,
　　2d Battalion, 35th Infantry, 4th Infantry Division. On 7 March
　　1969, as Company B was proceeding up the side of a hill, they were
　　suddenly engaged by an intense barrage of enemy automatic weapons
　　fire. Reacting immediately, Sergeant Balzarini led his squad from
　　the rear element through the area of contact in order to place sup-
　　pressive fire on the enemy. With only a minimum area of cover,
　　Sergeant Balzarini deployed his squad so as to relieve the intensity
　　of contact at the point element. During the maneuver, Sergeant
　　Balzarini was painfully wounded but continued to fight until the
　　enemy was routed. Sergeant Balzarini's outstanding leadership,
　　exceptional courage and exemplary devotion to duty are in keeping with
　　the highest traditions of the military service and reflect great credit
　　upon himself, his unit and the United States Army.
　Authority: By direction of the President, under the provisions of Executive
　　　Order 11046, 24 August 1962.

FOR THE COMMANDER:

OFFICIAL:
P. C. WEDDLE
CPT, AGC
Asst AG

DISTRIBUTION:
6 AVDDH-AGD
2 AVDDH-ASD
2 Indiv conc
1 Indiv's 201
5 2d Bn, 35th Inf

GORDON J. DUQUEMIN
Colonel, GS
Chief of Staff

1 CG, USARV, ATTN: AVHAG-DB,
  APO 96375
2 USA Pers Svc Support Center
  ATTN: AGPE-F, Fort Benjamin
  Harrison, Indiana 46249

The Bronze Star Citation Ted received for his actions on March 7, 1969.

front of me he was awake and conscious. He said, "Boy, was I ever praying that you weren't going to hit me." I hadn't known if he was alive or dead, but he had been shot in the stomach by the enemy, and still alive. I was so thankful that I had been especially careful not to hit him.

In Vietnam you see people get killed. You lose your best friends. Many lose arms or legs, and many survive. It's difficult to come to grips with the death of fellow veterans. It would have been easier to die myself than live with what I have seen.

There was a three-day stand down. (Kind of like a break in a safe area where you could clean up, get a hot meal, write a letter home, and to try to regroup and adequately get some rest.) We would have a hot meal and as much cold beer as we could drink. It was very dusty. The dust was almost knee deep. It probably hadn't rained for several months. We would be entering the monsoon season soon.

A chaplain was there to hold a ceremony for the dead. I remember standing there with tears in my eyes. Everyone had tears in their eyes. It was the first opportunity I had to mourn and stop to think about the men we had lost. It was not pleasant. It was very sad.

Later we were given hot meals and there was a kind of cattle trough filled with cold cans of beer. We drank a lot and didn't leave that trough. Several days later we were re-supplied and sent back out.

Ted writing home. Mail was important to vets.

I do remember a few good times. One was with my good buddy Carl, whose nickname was Pixie.

Carl and I grew up in a little town called Palmer, Michigan. We had a lot of fun growing up together in a little mining town where there wasn't much to do. Carl was fun to be with. He was smart and witty and kept me in stitches most of the time.

We were both in our second year of college and we knew that our draft number would be coming up soon so we both decided to sign up and get it over with. Carl signed up for the army in February and one month later I signed up. I didn't see him again until I was in Vietnam. I had communicated with him by mail while I was in training and once in a while would get a letter from him. He went through basics and a kind of clerk training and was shipped off to Vietnam. He became a company clerk on a great big base camp. I remember that he had a patch on him that was called the "leaning shit house."

I was wounded during the firefight on March 7, 1969. I received shrapnel from a rocket-propelled grenade (RPG) and couldn't walk because the impact of the rocket threw us down a hill and caused some injuries. It took several days of physical therapy before I was able to become ambulatory again. I was pretty burned out at about this time and my buddy Carl's outfit was just outside of Quin Nhon. I had called Carl to let him know I was in the hospital, and he had come to visit me. A week

My friend Carl in Vietnam.

later when I was released from the hospital he came back and we went downtown into the city and did some bar hopping. We stayed a little too late and by the time we got to the outskirts of town it was getting dark. A guy gave us a ride for a ways on a Lambretta, a small motor scooter. When we got off it was still ten miles through winding roads and rice paddies.

About ten minutes later I began to think. I was glad that Carl had a gun with him, but he informed me that he didn't have any bullets with him. I asked him why and he said they were too heavy! He said, "I'm not carrying all that weight around just to go out drinking!" So I said, "Gimme that gun! You probably don't even know how to shoot!" As it turned out there was only one clip in the gun. Luckily a deuce and a half (a two and a half ton truck) came by and picked us up. We crawled into the back of the truck, which took us right to Carl's base camp.

Carl asked his first sergeant if it was okay if I stayed there awhile to recuperate. I was supposed to go back to Pleiku and had my orders. But his sergeant said I could stay as long as I wanted, and I was burned out. So I stayed for a couple of days.

The guys on that base were required to wear steel pots on their heads and that's all I had was my boonie hat. Everyone was complaining that they had to wear steel pots and why was it that I could wear that boonie hat. The sergeant told them that I was infantry, and they weren't, that's why!

Carl and I spent some good time together. We went to the NCO club and got some beer. You weren't allowed to take beer outside of the club unless they were opened. So we had them open up a case of beer, every can, and we took it to some bleachers, drank warm beer, and watched the war. There were helicopters coming in and gun ships shooting in the distance. You could see the red tracers in between the live ammo. Eventually we went back to Carl's barracks and crashed. We had just fallen asleep when there was an alert and we had to go and sit in his office for safety until the alert was over with.

It was so hot and we were just dying from the heat. Carl shared a barracks with about 30 other guys and he had a bunk there and a little refrigerator. So on the way back to the barracks, hot and thirsty, he told me that he had one cold beer in his refrigerator waiting for him and he couldn't wait to drink it. When I informed him that I had already drank it he said, "What? You drank it? I was saving that!" I asked, "For what?" He said, "For now!"

I stayed with Carl for two or three days and I told him I had to get back to my unit. But I couldn't go to the Air Force base

Guts and boonie hats—no personal protection.

with no orders. My orders for a plane ride back were several days old. I would have gotten hauled in to the hoosgow because I didn't have current orders. So we hung around the helicopter pad asking all the pilots where they were going. I finally found someone who was going to Pleiku and asked him for a ride. (If the helicopter had crashed no one would have known what happened to me.)

When I got back I got into all kinds of trouble for staying extra days and got my ass chewed out good by the headquarter's company commander. I was promptly sent back out into the field. (What more could they do to me, send me to Vietnam? Being sent to the field was punishment enough.) The chewing out really didn't do much good because the next time I was in the hospital (with ambiotic dysentery) I gave myself another three-day visit with Carl. When I came in on the chopper the CO just looked at me and shook his head.

It was worth all of it seeing my good buddy, Carl. I was burned out and those visits helped me survive the rest of the tour.

The officers (Rank) never came out to the field to promote people. However, one day a sergeant came out to the field to promote someone and he told me, "You are going to be the next person promoted in this company." That meant that I would be made an E6.

I was at a base camp in the process of getting ready to go home (back to the United States). The company clerk came looking for me. He told me that the general had E6 stripes for me. I was told to get a driver and go out to this place called the Oasis, which was about eight to ten miles away, because that's where I was to meet the general. I got a driver and as we were on the road we came upon an accident. A deuce and a half had hit a Lambretta and injured some people. There was a lot of moaning, hysteria, and turmoil at the accident site and people were checking out and tending the people in the accident. A woman came up to me and held out her baby as if she were trying to tell me, "Take my baby." She was obviously very worried about the child. So I took the child in my arms, although he seemed to be okay. He was about a year old.

We took the baby and drove to the Oasis and instead of meeting the general we drove to an infirmary. I carried the baby inside and we told the doctor and nurse what had happened. We didn't know the baby's name or anything about him. The doctor took the child to examine him and we told him I was en route to meet this general and so we left the infirmary.

When we finally got to the correct place, the people said the general who would have promoted me was gone. So we turned around and went back to the base camp. I never did receive the promotion and eventually left the country, but at the same time we did the right thing and the baby was all the better for it. As a United States soldier I felt that many times we did the right thing—to look after your fellow man. We were tough when we had to be tough and yet we showed compassion and kindness when it was needed.

Milly's Story

While Ted was gone I wrote to him every day. I would race home from work each evening to see if there was a letter from him. The letters I received were dirty and smudged with red dirt. He would talk about the future and how much he missed everyone but seldom talked about what life was like in Vietnam. He spent the majority of the year in "the boonies" as he referred to them and talked about the elephants, tiger trails or snakes he saw. I could only imagine what he was going through. At one point he became very sick from drinking bad water and was diagnosed with a severe case of dysentery and an ulcerated intestine. He was told that he would be sent to Japan because there was no medication to treat it with in country. But just before receiving orders to be sent out they found some medication. He was treated with a medication that had arsenic in it to kill the parasite causing all of his problems. He was then sent back to the field to his unit. He was extremely thin and he dreaded going back to his unit.

Ted with ambiotic dysentery.

During that year he had two R & Rs. One was in Hawaii, where his mother and her best friend and I met him, and one was in Australia. When he stepped off of the bus in Hawaii's Fort DeRussey I barely recognized him. His brown hair was now blonde and he was extremely tan. Seeing him was wonderful! We swam in the ocean and lay on the beach in the warm sun. We drank Mai Tai's and ate coconut and pineapple every day. Hawaii was like a paradise. We loved the beauty of Hawaii and Diamond Head with the moon shining on the ocean at night. But as each day passed it was getting closer to the time we had to say goodbye and Ted would have to leave once more.

One night as we stood on the veranda watching the ocean a firecracker went off. It must have been a Hawaiian holiday. Ted reacted immediately, almost jumping off of the balcony. We were 16 floors up in the Hilton Hawaiian Village. It was a good indication of the hypervigilance he was experiencing living every day in the jungle. My heart was breaking the day he had to leave Hawaii. Our planes were traveling in opposite directions and it would be another three months before I would see him again. I prayed that he would be safe.

During the next few weeks Ted had led his company to an area where another company was being attacked by the Viet Cong. They had been hit by rocket fire and there were casualties and personnel that were wounded. They held the enemy at bay for hours and after the intensity of the battle was over Ted was medivaced to a hospital for treatment of shrapnel wounds. In two weeks he was back in the field. We knew very little of his experiences, his close brush with death, the injuries and death that he saw. He cooked soup in a beer can and mixed the Kool-Aid we'd sent him with the river water. They were supposed to use purification tablets but it made the water taste so bad that they didn't always use them. We were unaware what life was like for him because his letters didn't reflect any of it.

Everywhere they went there were booby-traps set by the Viet Cong. And there were snakes and it was usually around 90 to 100 degrees during the day and went down to 75 at night. In the rainy season it was hot and humid and they carried heavy backpacks filled with ammunition, food, pen and paper, and a blanket. In addition, each man carried eight quarts of water. They traveled nine miles a day in the heat. At times it was steep and mountainous and on those days they only covered about four miles. Survival was a daily exercise and you honed your skills daily. Ted was a platoon leader and was responsible for other lives.

At home we would watch the evening news with Walter Cronkite every night hoping that the troops would be sent home, praying that Ted was safe. It eventually ended for his parents and me when we found out Ted was finally coming home. It was finally over. But the war hadn't ended for Ted. He had been programmed and trained for war and when he came home he wasn't the same person.

As happy as Ted was to be at home, there was a veil between us. Ted drank heavily and smoked heavily and drove his car recklessly, like a bat out of hell. He bought a big motorcycle and he and his best friend, another Vietnam veteran, drove it to town to the bars and came home drunk, driving like there was no tomorrow. He slept with a gun next to his bed and would jump at any little noise. Our plans of marriage were put on a back burner. He barely spoke of marriage, knowing that he wasn't fit to get married or do much of anything. He didn't feel like he was ready to live in a civilized community and he wasn't ready to deal with relationships.

Ted was a different person than when he had left. The Army had taken him out of the jungles of Vietnam and within about three days had sent him to an army base in Washington and then home to the small town his parents lived in and he'd grown up in. He wasn't ready for this. He had lived a kind of life the past year that had programmed him to live a certain way with certain feelings, watching for the enemy, surviving. What I didn't realize was that there was an underlying anger underneath the surface. He lived in a state of vigilance, waiting for an attack or crisis, and was filled with anxiety. He was impatient, had bad dreams, night sweats and was abrasive with people. I would get angry with him because we would plan an evening together and he would be late and show up with three or four beers under his belt. There were times where he would come over and fall asleep on the couch and stay there all night long. It seemed that he wanted to spend his time in the bars rather than doing things with me. I should have known that he wasn't ready for marriage, but we had talked about it so much and I was tired of waiting to plan our wedding and the life we had talked about for so long.

In March 1971, the day after a blizzard, we were married in St. Paul's Catholic Church. There were huge snowbanks from the storm, but the sun was shining brightly. It was the first day of spring and the first day of our marriage. We had a beautiful reception and our families were there to share the day with us.

We had a small apartment on a second floor and some secondhand furniture. It was cute and cozy. Ted attended classes at Northern Michigan University under the GI Bill and I worked at the university as a secretary. We didn't have a lot of money but we were happy. Ted sold his motorcycle to pay off the payments on my car, and our rent was only $75.00 a month, so we were able to manage financially.

Seven months after we were married Ted got into a terrible car accident. He and a close friend had gone to Green Bay, Wisconsin, so his friend could have some dental surgery done. He needed a friend to accompany him in case he was drowsy when he came out of the dentist office. He too was a Vietnam veteran whom Ted had spent time with while they were stationed there. They had become close friends. On the way home from Green Bay they decided to look up another army buddy who was living in Wisconsin and the three of them had quite a bit to drink. They were only a few miles from home when they got into a terrible car accident. Ted was seriously injured. He had crushed several vertebrae in his back. He knew something was wrong when he heard the crack of his back. As he sat in the car he reached for the door handle, opened the door, and slowly rolled out onto the ground and waited for the ambulance to arrive. He spent the next agonizing month in pain in a circle bed that turned him over several times a day. He was in extreme pain and morphine did little to deaden the pain. His intestines stopped functioning and he was very seriously ill. One week after Ted's accident my doctor told me that I was pregnant.

The news of my pregnancy was unexpected, however it gave Ted reason and motivation to get well. He was very happy and it was a reason to go on. Each morning I would visit him at the hospital before I drove to work, and each evening after work I would sit at the hospital until 10 P.M. with him. I was exhausted but I knew how important it was to keep his spirits up. His recuperation period was long and painful but eventually he left the hospital able to walk with a big metal back brace on. We spent the next several weeks living with his parents.

We had been in the process of moving to a small house when Ted was injured in the accident. We had the house half painted inside and there was furniture and boxes everywhere. The oil burner which heated the house started on fire one day before we moved in and the fire department had to come and put the fire out and haul the burner out on the street. Ted's parents and several of his friends helped us to finish painting and putting furniture in place. Ted's mother wallpapered several rooms for us and his dad helped with the wiring and heating jobs. We were finally able to move into the house.

It was an old house that wasn't insulated very well and the bedrooms were upstairs. Ted wasn't able to climb stairs so we put a single bed in the living room for him to sleep on, across the room from the couch where I slept. His back brace kept him quite rigid and so each morning before I left for work I would have to put his socks on him. After I left for work his uncle, Donald, whom we loved dearly, came over and was like a guardian angel. He knew I was pregnant and didn't want me to have to shovel snow and would come over at 7 A.M. to make sure I could get my car out of the driveway. He would fix Ted breakfast and do the dishes. All day he would sit with him and keep him company. Before he left he would wash the kitchen floor, or vacuum the living room. Many times I would come home to find a big bowl of spaghetti that he had made all ready for dinner.

My mother would bring over homemade bread and biscuits. We had very little money to live on now that Ted wasn't attending school or getting the GI Bill. We lived on $300 a month which had to pay for groceries, rent, and heat and utilities. Our parents were very helpful during this time of our lives. Our fuel line that went to our oil burner had a slight wrinkle in it which created a dip, and the condensation would always freeze in that point when the weather was extremely cold. We would watch the flame go lower and lower until it was almost out. The window would be covered with frost on the inside, and Ted and I would huddle together under the quilts of his single bed until morning when we could call his father to come over with a torch to thaw out the line.

We survived that winter and Ted's back was healing well. On July 9, 1972, I gave birth to our first child. Her name was Angela Marie and she weighed 8 pounds and 2 ounces. She had dark hair and was absolutely beautiful. I had gone through a long labor and Ted sat by my side. At 6 A.M. our baby was finally born and we were ecstatic. Ted stood at the nursery window watching as they bathed and dressed her and suddenly broke down in tears and left the hospital to bring the good news to our parents.

One week later we took our baby girl home. Ted was very worried because he didn't have a job and I was only able to work until my seventh month of pregnancy. We had run out of money and we had another mouth to feed. I received many beautiful baby gifts and so I had almost everything I needed, but Ted needed to find a job and he was still in a back brace. He had worked as a bricklayer at one time but now his body would not allow him to do that type of work. Ted reluctantly applied for food stamps and we received $100 worth of groceries. He was embarrassed and made me promise I wouldn't tell anyone. A week later he received a call from a construction company saying that they had gotten his name from a supervisor. They had a job opening for a construction estimator in an office in Wausau, Wisconsin, and they would interview him for the job if he was interested. At that time we had exactly $30 to our name. He got the job and when Angie was five weeks old we moved to Wisconsin. Things were finally going well. Ted had a desk job, we had a nice apartment, a new baby, and financially we were able to hold our own. We loved our apartment. Everything was newly remodeled and our friends and family had helped us to move our furniture and belongings here. Ted loved his job, and every night he would come home and play with Angie.

Things had definitely worked out well except for one thing. Ted's mother had suffered a nervous breakdown. She had never really been able to realistically accept the fact that Ted was in Vietnam and pretty much lived in denial most of that year, putting it out of her mind and pretending he was at the neighborhood bar playing pool. When he came home she was so happy but she didn't want to let go, and so when we got married she was very disappointed. Soon after that Ted's sister got married right out of high school. Ted's back injury, the fact that both his sister and I were expecting babies, and

Ted's move 240 miles away from home became overwhelming. She began to suffer from a very severe depression and had to be hospitalized in Rochester, Minnesota. After a series of medication and shock therapy she finally recovered but was never a mentally healthy person after that. Ted felt a lot of guilt for moving away, yet he had to go where there was a job.

For the rest of his mother's life, 25 years, we dealt with bouts of depression, suicide attempts, and visits to psychiatric hospitals and nursing homes. From time to time she would be well enough to live at home for a few months, but she wouldn't take her medication and would slowly regress again and return to the hospital. She was eventually diagnosed with schizophrenia and severe depression. She was also bipolar.

It was heartbreaking for Ted. He loved his mother very much and it killed him to see her so ill. He spent many days traveling either to the Mayo Clinic with her or to hospitals to visit her over the years. The tragedy of her illness was that she was being diagnosed at a time when they knew very little about mental illness. Each time she got medical attention it seemed that the doctors were more confused than the time before. There were no support groups to help or deal with this and it was devastating to the whole family. Each time we would leave with a heavy heart because she would beg him not to leave and hated the fact that we lived in Wisconsin. Considering that Ted had an undiagnosed case of post-traumatic stress disorder, this whole situation and life in general was difficult to say the least.

On July 18, 1973, our second child was born. We named her Teresa. She had strawberry blonde hair and weighed 9 pounds 8 ounces. She was beautiful and she and Angie, being so close in age, were almost like twins. We had made some good friends and life was good, except that Ted wasn't himself lately. He'd had a physical and the doctor told him that his triglycerides were high and that he needed to restrict certain foods in his diet. He needed to eat less flour and starchy products and more fruits and vegetables. Ted adhered to the diet and began to lose weight. He also began to get edgy and irritable. He would snap at me for no reason at all. It was like his whole body chemistry was changing. What I didn't realize was that his thyroid gland was beginning to become overactive.

When Teresa was ten months old we moved back to Michigan. The company that Ted was working for was relocating to Minneapolis. We had a choice of moving to Minnesota with them or going back home. Ted felt that with his mother's illness, his father was living with a tremendous amount of stress and he wanted to be near him to help out. So we moved back to Marquette where Ted enrolled once again at Northern Michigan University to work on his degree in business administration. His back had healed and was strong enough so he could work with the bricklayers on weekends and in the summer months. He also decided to grow Ginseng (a medicinal herb) which he learned about while living in Wisconsin. We bought a two family home and rented out the upstairs apartment for the amount of our house payment. We received the GI Bill along with whatever Ted earned building basements with a friend in the summer months.

He worked night and day. During the winter he would work on construction during the day and attend classes at NMU at night. He was so tired that at times he fell asleep in class. After class he would come home and read his textbooks and fall into bed exhausted. On weekends, if he wasn't building a basement for someone he was working at our ginseng garden, picking weeds or putting up roofs, or spraying. After working at the garden he would stop at the VFW for a sauna, have a few drinks on an empty stomach, and came home drunk. He was getting thinner by the day and was seldom at home.

He eventually got his degree from NMU and was hired in the campus development office. The people at work would tease him about the amount of food he could eat and kept getting thinner. When everyone at work was on water diets, Ted would eat three meals a day and pie, ice cream cones and donuts all day at work. His coworkers were not losing a pound and Ted kept getting thinner. He was also getting more irritable and we would get into arguments frequently. He was a workaholic, working at the university by day and in the ginseng gardens in the evenings and on weekends. He was drinking more and we were also arguing more.

Several months after he began working at NMU we found out that I was pregnant for our third child. Our present house would not be big enough for all of us and it was not in a good neighborhood. We put the house on the market and as soon as it sold we moved in with my mother temporarily and bought a lot to build a new home.

Ted was under a great deal of stress. He worked during the day and cleared the lot for the house or worked on our new home at night. His mother's mental health was at its worst. She was agitated, unhappy and unreasonable and would call us many times a day. She would call Ted at work and insist upon talking to him. He was getting thinner and more tired and upset by the day. A mental illness is a very difficult thing to live with. When we would visit his mother she would pace back and forth and would be short of breath and desperate. She would never voluntarily sign herself into a hospital. It was when she was at her very worst, either a danger to herself, to others, or unable to care for herself, that Ted and his dad were able to have her committed. Eventually she was committed to a long-term facility 100 miles away for many months. Meanwhile Ted was dealing with multiple problems in his life, and PTSD didn't exactly help him to cope. He was filled with sadness and guilt. Christmas, and most holidays, were extremely difficult for him.

This illness had taken its toll on everyone in the family in one way or another. Ted's father was suffering from heart problems and Ted worried about him and the damage the stress was doing to his health. I was having nightmares, dreaming that his mother was ill and kidnapping my new baby. Ted was literally physically exhausted from work, from building a house, from the stress of his mother's illness, and what we didn't realize at the time, from a severe case of hyperthyroidism.

On October 22, 1977, our third child, Kristina, was born. She was so cute! She weighed 9 pounds, 7 and a half ounces. She had very little hair and her eyes were dark. I knew that I had finally had my brown-eyed baby. Three months later we moved into our new home. It was a beautiful four-bedroom, two story home with a big family room, a fireplace and a two car garage. We had a nice big yard in a nice neighborhood. Angie was five and in kindergarten and loved school. We should have been happy, but Ted was getting more unpredictable and impatient by the week. He would get angry if the children made too much noise, and would jump if there was a loud noise. The girls had to play quietly and had to be well behaved. They didn't dare cause any problems, and in years to come it almost became an obsession to make Dad proud.

Ted would not only blow up at me but at store clerks and at work. He couldn't sleep at night and what I wasn't aware of was that he would go downstairs and drink a glass of brandy or gin so that he could fall asleep. His legs would shake in his sleep and his hands shook during the day. He was six feet, one inch tall and weighed 140 pounds. He was impossible to wake up in the morning and was always late for work. He kept getting upper respiratory infections and was warned that if he didn't stop smoking he was one step away from lung cancer.

I finally talked to our doctor and he arranged a thorough physical for Ted. He diagnosed Ted with a severe case of hyperthyroidism. His heart rate was 135 at rest and he could have had a heart attack. He was put on medication and immediately began to feel his body slowing down. The doctor told him it was like having a car in neutral and having the gas pedal to the floor 24 hours a day. He was lucky he hadn't become psychotic. He was lucky he still had a marriage and a job. He had been so hyper that if he couldn't find something in a store he was rude to the store clerks, and at home he was impossible to live with at times.

Now things would be better, or so I thought. After two years his thyroid went in the opposite direction. He began to get tired and cold and irritable and learned that his thyroid had stopped functioning. He was put on Synthroid and began to feel much better. Once again I thought my troubles were over.

Thyroid problems are seen often in Vietnam veterans. I am not sure why. However, it is a typical problem. A defoliator called Agent Orange was sprayed on the trees in Vietnam and many veterans have been affected by the chemicals. Many have developed cancer and other very serious physical health problems.

Although Ted's major symptoms of shaking (tremors) and weight loss (or gain) were gone, the moodiness and anger were still there. I was sure when his thyroid was treated that the anger would be gone. His coworkers had nicknamed him Little Hitler and I joked with our doctor that at times he was a Jekyll and Hyde.

The doctor told me he suspected that Ted's behavior was a stress reaction. He had known many Vietnam veterans and they all acted the same and had many of the same problems. I didn't know what to do with that information. Ted should probably have counseling but he hated psychiatrists because of his experience with his mother. (He often said they should put all the psychiatrists in a bag and throw them into Lake Superior!) In the state of mind he was in I didn't dare suggest psychological help. And so life went on and we all walked on eggs not wanting to provoke him or make him angry.

When he was happy he was a kind, loving husband and father. He had a great sense of humor and would make us laugh. He would play monopoly and cards with the kids, watch Little House on the Prairie with them and give them piggyback rides. During the summer we would spend time at the lake at our cottage and the girls would swim. We had bonfires at night where they would roast hot dogs and marshmallows. The girls loved their father very much, but they were also very much affected by his anger and his moods. He would blow up at them over the littlest things such as not hanging up their jackets. On one occasion he threw all of their jackets out the front door. Even the dog would get nervous. While doing our taxes Ted became so frustrated and angry that he threw the plastic bill box on the floor, sending the dog running, and shaking, into the living room. The girls just sat quietly petting the dog and stayed out of sight. If someone dropped something accidentally he would holler at them for carelessness.

He was extremely jumpy these days and was known to have thrown the cat out the front door into a snowbank if she was in his path. If someone accidentally got hurt he would holler at them and everyone else. He was controlling and had to know where everyone was and what they were doing. Heaven help us if a car backfired or a firecracker exploded. We had many arguments over his behavior, which didn't help matters at all. He would worry constantly about matters at work and seemed to be anxious or upset most of the time. To top it off his mother was at her very worst. She would call 20 times a day crying and screaming in the phone from the hospital. If Ted told her to stop calling and hung up she would call back. We had to get an unlisted number, which she eventually got anyway. The kids and I began to shield him from these calls by answering the phone all the time and telling her he wasn't home. We ended up having to deal with her behavior which made us nervous and upset. I was gaining weight and my blood pressure was going up. I dealt with life's problems through food and it was taking its toll. Who knows what it was doing to our daughters.

Ted got his master's degree in planning and public administration in 1983. His father was so proud and Ted couldn't wait to have his father attend graduation to see him receive the degree. One week before his graduation ceremony his father died of a heart attack. He'd had an arrhythmia and his heart just stopped one day while opening up a can of paint at camp. The neighbors found him dead and called the ambulance. Ted was devastated and could barely get through the funeral. He had seen friends get killed in Vietnam and he had to try to let it go, but this was someone he dearly loved and protected. He had been there for Ted no matter what and now he had lost his best friend. He felt a lot of anger towards his mother and all of the problems she'd had. The stress of it all had killed his dad. He and his dad had become very close and they did everything together the past few years.

The depression that Ted felt that day didn't leave him. He began to feel that life was too hard. He remembers riding around the NMU campus on one occasion thinking that he needed to end it all. He was getting harder and harder to live with. He was becoming verbally abusive and had trouble coping at work. I didn't know if I could live like this any longer. I didn't want my kids to live in an unhappy family. And yet a part of me knew that deep down Ted loved us and couldn't help the way he was. I finally talked to our doctor and convinced Ted to go in to talk to him. He was diagnosed with depression and put on medication. I was so relieved. I was sure that everything would finally be okay. This was the problem, and now it was finally solved. He would take an antidepressant and he would get well.

The medication helped a lot. Ted was a happier person and seemed to cope much better with life. Our girls were good kids and did well in school. Life definitely had improved. But we still occasionally saw an underlying anger in him. He would wake up angry most mornings and it was always just under the surface, ready to emerge.

While the girls were in school I attended classes at NMU and finally got my degree in writing/speech with a minor in elementary education. I felt good, like I had really accomplished something important. It was good for my self-esteem and I hoped that I was a good role model for my children. Except for the birth of my daughters it was the most memorable day of my life. I was able to obtain a part time job teaching and working with developmentally disabled adults. I loved my job and because it was only part time I still had lots of time to spend with my kids. My students were sweet and kind and I grew to love them. I worked with English Second Language students and people who had problems with reading and wanted to improve their skills. I didn't have a full time job, didn't get the kind of pay they did, and wondered if I was considered beneath other teachers in the work world until a nun at the school stopped by one day to visit and told me I was doing "God's work." I never worried about status again. I was indeed doing God's work. And I loved every minute of it.

Ted's mother spent years in a nursing home when she was finally stable enough to leave the hospital, Time had healed a lot of wounds. We visited her frequently and took her out for meals. Ted had finally put the past behind him and decided that he needed to have a good relationship with his mother for her sake as well as his. Living with anger damages your health and eats away at you. Forgiveness is healing. He missed his father terribly and wanted to do things right. We would plan mini vacations for our family at the Keweenaw Peninsula, a beautiful place in Northern Michigan where we would stay in rustic cabins with a fireplace and picnic on the beaches of Lake Superior. We would take the kids horseback riding and out for ice cream cones. On weekends we would spend time at our summer cottage swimming and enjoying the summer.

No matter how hard he tried, however, Ted's obsessiveness, anger, and impatience always seemed to surface and his unpredictable behavior made the girls hesitant to have their friends over at our house. If they giggled too loud, left their shoes in the way, held the door open too long, or talked on the phone too long he would get angry and reprimand them. It didn't matter who was there. His mother's incessant phone calls made him hate the phone and when it rang he would panic. One day when the phone rang one too many times he ripped it out of the wall and threw it down the basement stairs. Another time it landed in the garbage can. He couldn't deal with anything else, much less the phone. The rage he felt inside was not only alarming to his family, but also to him.

Ted began to get reclusive. He would sit in the family room watching TV for hours not wanting to be disturbed. He was drinking alcohol more and eating compulsively. On weekends in the fall, he would pack up the dog and go to our camp and spend the whole weekend alone. It was a kind of refuge from the world and he felt safe there. He usually drank too much and spent a lot of time stewing about things and trying to solve problems. When he was at home he would sit in the sauna basking in the warmth and stewing about things that happened at work. I suspected that thoughts of suicide were on his mind.

One day as we were coming out of one of the local stores an old friend who was a Vietnam veteran was also walking out and he and Ted began to talk. Ted was happy to see him and asked how he was doing. The guy mentioned that he had started a Vietnam veterans support group and he invited Ted to attend any time. It met on Wednesday nights. I remember thinking that maybe he should give it a try, but didn't say anything, and Ted didn't attend until years later. Then he would meet many other friends who were living with the same problems and would help him.

Over the years he had been reprimanded at work for his abrasiveness towards other coworkers. He was having a very difficult time coping with life and particularly with work. At one point his job was reduced to three-quarters time as Director of Labor Ed. He had a whole new job to learn and a new learning curve. He was told there were budget cuts, and it was three-quarters time or retirement. He was too young to retire and we would have no health insurance. At his age where would he find another job? And so he continued on at the university but was extremely depressed and angry and talked about getting even with some of his supervisors. He was having a difficult time functioning at work and he didn't want to get out of bed in the morning. He would wake up extremely depressed and had a hard time beginning his day and functioning. Finding something to wear was a chore, and everything was a big effort.

He worked hard at his job but he was unsure of himself and resentful towards authority figures at work. (Resentment towards authority figures is a symptom of PTSD and many of the veterans I spoke with felt the same way.) When he would pack up and go to camp on the weekends I would worry about him. He was becoming more and more reclusive. Camp and the woods was something he loved, but I knew that there were thoughts of suicide in the back of his mind.

Considering the turmoil in our home at times, my daughters did well in school, were active in church and were nice kids. They had a nice home, a cat and a dog, and lots of friends. However, everything was a big deal at our house; everything was a crisis. It wasn't like that at their friends' houses, and their fathers were so different. They didn't have to walk on eggs or deal with unpredictable behavior.

On June 30, 2003, Ted was finally able to retire. There were budget cuts and his program was going to be cut. He would either have to bump someone else out of a job or retire, and he chose retirement. We could somehow manage. I could get insurance through my job and with his retirement check we could survive. I was relieved. Now maybe his troubles were over. He wouldn't have to deal with work. He could fish and hunt and not worry about work. We wouldn't be wealthy by any means but we could make it. All of our kids were out of college and had moved to Minneapolis and gotten good jobs. Angie had two degrees, one in psychology and one in occupational therapy. Teresa had a degree in nutrition and was working for a pharmaceutical company. Kristina had a degree in communications and was also working for a pharmaceutical company. They were all happy. Angie and Teresa had wonderful husbands and Angie was expecting our first grandchild. Ted had the best of everything in this world. He had struggled for years and now he could relax. He had always teased me and asked when I was going to take care of him. Now I would continue to work part-time and I would get insurance and take care of him.

Ted still wasn't happy. He would explode in anger and he drank and ate too much. Something inside of him was eating away at him. Now that he had time to enjoy life I thought he would finally fish and hunt, but he didn't enjoy anything. He was still isolating himself, still jumpy, and still waiting for the crisis. We never forgot the time our youngest daughter walked into the room and he was startled and he had poked her in the throat with his fingers, a kind of vital thrust, and an army survival tactic. (An exaggerated startle response.) He'd felt so bad and apologized to her several times. At night he dreamed that he was being sent back to Vietnam and he would wake up in a cold sweat. He needed help but he had no faith in the mental health field. In the back of his mind he thought he was going crazy.

Things were getting progressively worse. He had a great family, a beautiful home, a cottage on a lake, a retirement income and several really true friends he could talk to, and he was still a very unhappy person. It had gotten to the point where he didn't go out to camp alone anymore. I wondered why. It wasn't until recently that he told me he was afraid of what he might do. He also had brandy bottles lined up in the garage. He started out saving them for a friend who makes wine, but after emptying over fourteen bottles, not counting all of the beer he had been drinking, he began to see that he was self-medicating and had a problem.

It was at about this time that I saw the program on television about PTSD. Those men were describing my husband! And they all had the same problems, the same story. They were all Vietnam veterans.

When I felt the time was right I had a talk with Ted one afternoon. I told him that I thought I finally understood what was wrong. I told him about the program I had watched on TV and that I thought he had the same symptoms as the men on that program. I explained that I had a phone number he could call for help if he wanted it. We looked up PTSD on the computer and read all of the symptoms. He let out a sigh and said, "I have every one of them." He left the room and went out into the garage and drank a beer. When he came in he looked at me and said, "If you promise to come with me I'll go for help." That afternoon I called the number and by the end of the day we had an appointment with a therapist in the area who works with Vietnam veterans. He would see Ted in a couple of days.

The day we went to the therapist we were both a little nervous. When we got there we had to fill out some forms and answer a lot of questions. I asked Ted the questions and he gave me the answers to mark down. When the therapist finally came to meet us, he introduced himself and explained that he would be doing an assessment to decide whether or not Ted actually suffered from post-traumatic stress disorder. He said that it would be better if Ted came in alone and that I could come back for him in two hours.

Ted wanted me to go in with him for moral support but the therapist explained that he would be talking about some things

Ted & Milly with grandchildren three years after diagnosis and counseling.

that he might not want anyone else to know about. They would be talking about Vietnam. So I left, and when I returned Ted was walking out of the office with a smile on his face looking very relieved. He liked his therapist, Dan, and for the first time in a long time he felt that there was hope. He would have one more long appointment with Dan and then I would be allowed to go to his appointments with him.

After his therapist's evaluation he was sent to Milwaukee to the veteran's hospital for an appointment with a psychiatrist there. That evaluation would then be sent to Detroit to be evaluated by doctors there. It was the consensus of all of the evaluations that Ted indeed suffered from chronic PTSD with major depression. Because of the severity of the depression he was also considered unemployable. His level of concentration impairment, his irritability, his discomfort in social situations, and his difficulty with authority figures were all a part of his symptoms. He had feelings of detachment or estrangement from others, and a sense of a foreshortened future. I had always wondered why he kept telling me where all of our important papers were kept and if anything happened to him what I should do and who I should go to for help. He experienced low energy, low self-worth, had suicidal thoughts and sleep disturbances. These were just some of the problems uncovered by his assessment and evaluation.

The doctor advised him to double his antidepressant and prescribed an anxiety medication for times when he suffered from anxiety. He would be required to attend one-on-one therapy as well as group therapy. He was advised to limit his intake of alcohol, which he had used to self-medicate for years. Ted also joined a Vietnam support group meeting once a week. He has telephone numbers of all of the people there he can choose to call if he needs to talk to someone.

The veterans at these meetings have been extremely supportive and caring and he has finally found someone who understands how he feels and what he has gone through. He now wants to help other veterans who are in need of help. He

Ted on the Purple Heart Trail shortly after being diagnosed with PTSD
and getting some counseling.

has learned so much about his problem and the triggers that send him back to Vietnam. He knows that things like watching the news, hearing '60s music, different sights and sounds, hot humid weather, or a helicopter hovering overhead can all send him back to Vietnam, where all of the fears and feelings come back. He is learning how to cope with these things and has become educated about the ways he can overcome some of his symptoms.

Ted came home from Vietnam in 1970 with a Purple Heart, a Bronze Star and many other medals. We, his family, thought that his war was over and we could put this behind us. However, Ted never left the war. For 35 years he has lived with the trauma and experiences, haunted in his dreams. It had changed him and almost destroyed his life, his marriage and his relationships with his children and anyone who knew him. Now he is on the road to recovery. After a year and a half of therapy, and support from his fellow veterans, he now is feeling happier and looks forward to the future. He will continue with therapy for a long time to come.

Ted will never be the same person he was before Vietnam. He will always have triggers that will cause him to overreact to situations. Recently we took a trip to Las Vegas. While we were there Ted was uncomfortable, irritable, and was not enjoying

---

C I T A T I O N

BY DIRECTION OF THE SECRETARY OF THE ARMY
THE ARMY COMMENDATION MEDAL

is presented to

SERGEANT THEODORE BALZARINI, ███████ UNITED STATES ARMY
Company B, 2d Battalion, 35th Infantry
4th Infantry Division

who distinguished himself by exceptionally meritorious service in support of allied counterinsurgency operations in the Republic of Vietnam. During the period January 1969 to January 1970 while serving as a Squad Leader he astutely surmounted extremely adverse conditions to obtain consistently superior results. Through diligence and determination, he invariably accomplished every task with dispatch and efficiency. His unrelenting loyalty, initiative and perseverance brought him wide acclaim and inspired others to strive for maximum achievement. Selflessly working long and arduous hours, he has contributed significantly to the success of the allied effort. His commendable performance was in keeping with the finest traditions of the military service and reflects distinct credit upon himself and the United States Army.

Citation for Ted's Army Commendation Medal.

the vacation at all. We wondered why he was acting the way he was. It turned out that there were crowds of people everywhere, and a good majority of the people were Asian. Later we realized that this was a trigger that brought back feelings of Vietnam, a time that he was living in a survival mode.

Another vacation he took was to Colorado, to Elk hunt. It was a trip he had planned for with one of his best friends, and looked forward to for years. As he carried his rucksack and a rifle through the mountains, it was a constant reminder of the Chuprong Mountains of Vietnam. He continually had to remind himself that he was on a wild animal hunt and not a search and destroy mission. It was another time that there were triggers and constant reminders of his experiences in Vietnam. After two days of carrying a rucksack and rifle he traded them in for his camera and spent the remainder of vacation enjoying the beauty and nature of Colorado. He isn't sure whether he will give Elk hunting another try. However, the mountains and the camaraderie and the beauty of the area turned out to be a surreal experience. The trekking through the mountainous black forest gave an uneasy feeling of times past and was very disappointing to him.

Symptoms of PTSD

What is post-traumatic stress disorder (PTSD)? It is a stress reaction to trauma. For some people it is the aftermath of a rape, a tragic death, a car accident, or a traumatic experience in life. For the combat veteran and for my husband, it was the result of a year in Vietnam. There are many young men suffering from post-traumatic stress disorder in the United States who are not aware that there is such a thing and that it has affected them as a result of war, whether it be the Vietnam, Korean, Desert Storm, World War II, Iraq or any other war.

While the symptoms for PTSD may differ slightly for each person, the most common symptoms, many of which you'll notice showed up in my husband Ted, are listed below.

- Anxiety
- Impatience
- Anger—explosiveness

- Workaholism
- Irritability—unpredictability
- Obsessiveness
- Alcohol or drug abuse
- Hopelessness
- Paranoia—worry
- Negativity
- Isolation—reclusiveness
- Nightmares
- Depression—moodiness
- Suicidal thoughts
- Hypervigilance—jumpiness
- Avoidance
- Reckless behavior
- Intrusive thoughts
- Inability to cope with problems
- Helplessness
- Lack of concentration
- Passive-aggressive behavior

While interviewing veterans they all seemed to have a lot in common. Drinking and/or drug use, a way of self-medicating, became a problem. Relationships with others became a problem. They felt distant, like they didn't really fit in anymore, except with other combat veterans. They all had nightmares and intrusive thoughts. Thoughts of war and Vietnam entered their thoughts every day and at times never went away. Most have feelings of mistrust, not even trusting themselves at times due to an inner rage that is always under the surface. All of the veterans I spoke with said that they were reclusive. They spent a great deal of time alone and wish they lived away from everything. They have feelings of guilt and ask, "Why did I make it back to the world and my buddy didn't?" They avoid all emotional attachments and hold back most feelings. They are numb and feel dead inside. This affects their marriage, friendships, and jobs.

Of course, most Vietnam veterans came back and adjusted well to life at home. Ordinarily people heal, and in time most situations are dealt with and we go on with our lives. It is normal to experience some trauma. But in some people, the horrors of war are not healed over time. Experiencing delayed stress reactions and having readjustment problems, they remember and relive the trauma, struggling with mental health problems for the rest of their lives. For these veterans the horrors of war are as vivid today as they were many years ago when they first experienced them. While initially happy that they had survived and were able to return home safely, nine to thirty months after being discharged they began to feel the effects of post-traumatic stress disorder. What they had gone through in the war would affect them, and remain with them, for the rest of their lives. It had left its scar on them.

The average age of the American Soldier was 19.2 years, much younger than participants in earlier wars. After seeing many of their fellow soldiers wounded or killed, it caused a kind of rage within them. At the time it happened they had to think very quickly and fight for their own survival—they had no time to grieve. But the anger and helplessness remained in them, repressed somewhere in the subconscious. Later it would come out as anger, usually at innocent people, most often at wives, children and family members.

Post-traumatic stress disorder not only affects veterans of war, but rape victims, child abuse victims, sexual, physical and emotional abuse victims. It can affect someone who has been very ill, had a car accident, or witnessed a horrible illness or death. It has changed the lives of those who have lived through natural disasters such as earthquakes, hurricanes, tornadoes and floods. The families and survivors of 9/11 feel the effects of PTSD. The helplessness and fear that a person feels remains with them. A numbing defense mechanism takes over to prevent a breakdown associated with feeling the full impact of a tragedy or traumatic situation.

In his book, *The Trauma Spectrum: Hidden Wounds and Human Resiliency* (New York: W.W. Norton & Company, 2005), Dr. Robert Scaer observes that trauma can be brought on by a life-threatening experience as well as a state of helplessness. This trauma actually affects the structure of our brains and can lead to dysfunctional physiological changes in both the body and the brain. If someone has been overly conditioned to threats on his or her life, the mind senses a warning or threat where none exists. Dr. Scaer terms this threat "imprisonment of the mind," because the mind has been frozen in the past and continually perceives a threat, resulting in emotional pain and sometimes, physical pain.

The classic diseases of stress, peptic ulcers, hypertension, and heart disease are shown in studies of wartime veterans and prisoners of war. In a state of terror or helplessness a person may involuntarily vomit, lose control of his bladder or bowels, or faint. It can also cause a person to experience emotional problems, sleep disturbances, intestinal problems and cognitive impairment.

Trauma has also been connected to Fibromyalgia and chronic fatigue syndrome with symptoms including skeletal pain, points of tenderness on the body, a glue-like morning stiffness, fatigue, and interrupted, non-restorative sleep. Symptoms may also include such things as numbness, tingling, hypervigilance, emotional instability, dizziness, dry mouth and eyes, irritable bowel syndrome, gastro-esophageal reflux problems, and inflammation of the bladder, suggesting that these symptoms originate in the brain.

Here are some of the symptoms as described by the veterans in their own words.

I can't concentrate. I lose my temper easily. I have major flashbacks. At Halloween, I have a hard time with pumpkins when they are smashed as they remind me of a head that had been split open. I can't get close to people because I don't trust them. I startle easily. I find myself looking for bunkers and traps while in the woods. Socially I am not comfortable. I am paranoid about people looking at me. I have bad nightmares. I don't sleep much at night. I try to stay away from people. I'm not comfortable around people. I can't stand out in the open, like waiting in line. I'm always looking and watching. I had a drinking problem.

My ability to tolerate bullshit is getting less and less. I don't take no shit from anyone who hasn't been to Vietnam. I have night sweats and bouts of anxiety. I can't sleep at night. I have a problem with my anger and irritability. I learned to trust only myself, not other people. I trusted the government at first but instead I was betrayed. There were demons in my soul when I got back. I felt dehumanized. I have trouble getting close to anyone. Emotionally, I feel numb. I think about Vietnam every day.

I'm sure my family really took its toll. I was so out of control. My alcohol use has been increasing. I have been kind of a control freak. I need to be better to my wife. I caused a lot of problems for her. It makes me feel bad that my wife and children don't have a better rapport with me because I was so explosive. Here I am a veteran and I'm all messed up.

I have nightmares nightly. I'm on edge. My wife recently left me. My life is plastic and fake. I drink nightly to get to sleep. I think about suicide. I have a .45 in my nightstand. I never mentioned a word about Vietnam for 33 years. I haven't been able to think, I can't focus. I have half finished work. My memory is poor and I can't sleep. I'm constantly on alert waiting for something to happen.

The Iraq war has been a constant trigger. I have no focus, diminished interests, no ambition. I have a reoccurring dream of being in the highlands. I'm in the middle of a patrol. I start walking around a tree and I feel a bullet penetrate my shoulder, then my right chest and then the middle of my chest. As I die I wake up. The fear is terrifying. It goes right to my core. It is right to my soul. There is always a feeling of shame, always a feeling of guilt, always the feeling of fear. When I smell dirt or diesel fuel I think about Vietnam. It was certainly different when I got back, no fanfare. Loud noises startle me.

Your brain starts to replay certain experiences and no matter what you want to think about, it doesn't stop. You see the blood, you hear the screaming, you see their faces and the tears, and you can't block it out.

You are always paranoid. You jump at loud noises and are in a constant state of hypervigilance where you are continually ready for a crises. You never really rest or calm down. Your adrenaline spikes on a moment's notice.

Every time you hear a chopper go over, or a fire-cracker goes off on the fourth of July, or the weather becomes stifling hot and humid, you are back in Vietnam. Your anger is just underneath the surface and you become angry at the littlest things, taking it out usually on the people you are the closest to. Eventually people want nothing to do with you because of your behavior. Even if you don't behave badly your family is always on guard and walking on eggs because you just might explode at any time.

Although most men never talk about it, post-traumatic stress disorder has been the source of trauma and problems in their lives for years after they return home. They bury it deep in their minds and souls, hopefully to forget. They suffer in silence and eventually it makes its way to the surface coming out as anger, alcohol or drug abuse, failed marriages, or failed careers, along with many of the other symptoms mentioned above. Some have learned to cope, but many are affected in some way.

Frequently the symptoms show up at retirement. When there is less to do and more time to think, these intrusive thoughts creep back into their minds and begin to create problems.

Because PTSD affects people in different ways in a variety of circumstances, I have included the experiences of several veterans from different wars, as well as my own story dealing with my husband as a Vietnam veteran, in the chapters that follow. These people have honestly opened up their personal lives to help others. You will see how war and its experiences have affected the lives of these men.

Post-Traumatic Stress Disorder from Soldiers in War

"When I was in Vietnam the guy sleeping next to me was attacked and eaten by a tiger. It still gives me nightmares. I wake up at night and see a tiger in the hallway."

A Vietnam veteran

Vietnam

Vietnam was a beautiful and dangerous place, all at the same time. In fact, it was its very beauty that hid its danger. Here's how one veteran remembers it.

If you could look beyond the war, Vietnam was beautiful. The triple canopies, the teakwood forests, and the majestic terrain features were all beautiful. The waterfalls, with microclimate exotic plants and flowers were awesome, as the mist sprayed from the waterfalls hydrated the existence of a special ecosystem. At the same time, you had to constantly look over your shoulder and you couldn't jeopardize your safety to enjoy the ambiance of this environment.

Most of the seacoast of Vietnam was made up of limestone. Shaped by the monsoon climates and heavily vegetated, it has unique and spectacular landforms.

The seacoast is called a karst region, which means it is made up of limestone. Due to the fact that it is water soluble it has many cavernous features and prominent terrain features.

The interior of Vietnam was drastically different. The farming regions were low flat lands and rice paddies. The Mekong Delta was the flood plain of the river that was emptying out into the ocean and was made up of silt and muddy areas from ages of erosion.

In the central part of South Vietnam there was more brush bush, the beginning of trees, and elephant grass. It consisted of a tangled, heavy ground cover and thick undergrowth.

The north was high country, the central highlands, or Chuprong Mountains. It is mountainous but fully vegetated. In this part of the country there were extremes in the weather. For six months of the year it was powder dry and the creeks would dry up. During the soggy rainy season it was like a torrent. It was like going from desert and red ants, termites and snakes, to the rain, bloodsuckers, and leaches. The ground becomes so saturated from the rains that it won't hold your body weight, so you're slipping and sliding. The decayed humus and plant material that was as hard as a brick becomes wet and slippery, like loonshit.

The possibilities of Cam Rahn Bay, the China Sea, and the seacoast places could actually be beautiful enough to be developed for recreation and vacation places that would be awesome. It has a climate that, for those who can afford to travel, would be appreciated. However, being under communist control and not having a tourist-friendly government, a treasure is lost. Entertaining the rest of the world with their beauty would have enhanced their economy. The seacoast of the South China Sea is every bit as beautiful as anyplace you might see in Florida. It might compare to Cancun or Aruba. There is a pristine kind of beauty.

However, for the United States veteran, it was not a place that could be remembered for its beauty.

Steve

Steve

He sat on the edge of his bed in nothing but his underwear, and in his hand was a nine-millimeter gun. His marriage had been destroyed. He was in total despair. He didn't want to face another day. He had thought about suicide many times before…but he couldn't do it because he didn't want to hurt his children. But today…today was so painful that nothing else entered his mind but ending it all. He didn't want to take another breath.

Steve had been in Vietnam with the Marine Corps from October 1967 to May 1969 as a radioman-field wireman. For years he had been haunted by his experiences and memories of Vietnam. He didn't want to remember, it was just there…every morning when he woke up. There were triggers that wouldn't let him forget. The sight of a dead deer brought the stench of rotting flesh. The smell of gunpowder or diesel fuel brought him back to a firefight. A day fishing in the woods took him to the jungles of southeast Asia, and even a pleasant dream could end with the face of an Asian soldier—a Gook, as they were referred to.

His wife couldn't deal with his lack of coping skills anymore. She was a wonderful woman, the love of his life. But he had immersed himself in work to the extent of neglecting his wife and family. She had spent so much time being lonely that her love for him had died. His pain and attempts to shut out the world had alienated the people he loved most of all. His businesses occupied all of his time and his mind. He didn't have to think or feel if he was busy and up to his ears in work. And now it had come to this.

The telephone began to ring. He looked at hit. "Shit!" he said. "Don't bother me!" he thought. He was going to kill himself. "What a f'n time for the phone to ring." He let it ring. It wouldn't stop. It just rang and rang and rang. Five, ten, twenty times it rang. Finally he grabbed the phone.

"Hello," he said. The person on the other end said he needed to talk to him. Could he meet him now, at the restaurant? "Hell, no! I'm in my underwear and ready for bed. Who is this?"

"This is Dan," the voice said. It was a friend he hadn't seen in many years. They had been in Vietnam together. Occasionally they had spotted each other on the highway and waved. They only lived a few miles from one another, but they never spoke. Dan had been severely injured in Vietnam and had a metal plate in his head. He'd had to take strong medications for years to live a half normal life. "I need to see you now," he said.

"Okay, I'll be right there," Steve replied. Then he thought, "Damn! What does he want?"

As Steve pulled into the almost empty parking lot of his restaurant he could see Dan standing in the entry waiting for him. There was an exit sign above him and the red light illuminated him. As Steve walked up to him, Dan extended his arms. As they hugged, Steve began to cry. There was a very special bond between them, an understanding that required no words.

They spent some time getting reacquainted and then Dan said he was going to pick him up at nine o'clock the next morning and they were going somewhere together. "Where?" Steve asked. "You'll see," Dan replied.

The next morning Dan persistently rang the doorbell until Steve answered. "Where are we going?" he asked. "You'll see," Dan answered once again.

That was the day Steve finally felt a glimmer of hope. He felt that spark to go on once more. They were at the veterans' clinic and they were talking to a psychologist. Steve had the option of staying in the hospital that night, as a safety precaution. However, after talking with the psychologist he had somehow gained enough strength and hope, and he would go home today.

During the next few weeks Steve saw the psychologist every Monday and Friday. On Wednesdays, Dan would take him to a Vietnam veterans support group meeting. In that first meeting he could only sit and listen, and choke back the tears, and eventually cry. Steve had really struggled over the years. He had nightmares and flashbacks; he felt like he really didn't fit in with other people. He felt so alone.

Soon another friend, who had also gone through a divorce, invited him to a divorce care group at a local church. Apprehensively, he attended his first meeting and met another group of people, friends, who would see his pain and help him to recover from the grief he felt. He began to attend church on a regular basis. Not the church he had grown up with, but another church. And it was there that he felt the love of God and he accepted Christ. He realized then that Dan's call was not

One of many "doodles" by Steve Wahlstom, a Vietnam veteran, since he began counseling.

just a coincidence. (Dan still isn't sure why he called that night when he did.) God had been watching over Steve and walking with him all the while. He just needed to let him into his life.

Steve suffers from post-traumatic stress disorder (PTSD). His experiences in Vietnam were, and still are, so ingrained in his mind that each day he still lives with the sensations, smells, fears, guilt, and anger that plague him.

A handsome, intelligent and caring man, Steve has owned his own business for years. Today he is finally finding happiness and peace. At times he still feels sadness and has bad days, and the triggers are still there that bring him back to the jungles and war, but thanks to many hours of counseling, group therapy and the bond and friendship of other veterans who understand, he is healing. He has learned coping skills and has received information that enables him to deal with the trauma and heartbreak yet live a normal life. His faith in God sustains him every day. He knows now that when he sees a dead deer lying on the side of the road that he will probably still smell human flesh. But now he knows why this happens and he can deal with it and continue on. He hopes to find a special relationship in his future. He values his friendship with his former wife and his children and takes each day as it comes. And he knows that God walks with him every day.

Tony

Tony

Tony was raised in Marathon City, Wisconsin. He was a radio relay operator in communications for the artillery in Vietnam. He was one of three communications persons of the United States Marines attached to army units that rotated in and out of a base called Gio Linh. The army units came and went but Tony was there for the duration. His experience in Vietnam has left deep invisible scars. Nightmares haunt him and he can no longer sleep more than a few hours a night. He thinks about Vietnam 12 to 20 hours per day. "It's like I've never left Vietnam," he says.

"In reality, I know I'm not there, but when I returned home I felt like a wild animal that wandered into civilization. I didn't feel like I belonged here."

Tony spent months in Vietnam in Gio Linh. It was a new firebase and they were sent there to build bunkers. The first few days were okay, but around the third day rounds began to hit the base. A United States convoy was coming in with artillery and was completely blown away. They were fired on all night, and it was reported in the Stars and Stripes newspaper that in excess of 1,100 rounds of artillery came in that night. The 20-acre compound looked more like a junkyard than a base. Out of 200 people, 40 men were injured or killed. That was just the beginning of his experience in Gio Linh.

As bad as that night was, the future was even worse. For the next five months they took 50 rounds a day. Tony felt like it would never end. He knew in his mind that he would never allow himself to become a prisoner. He always saved one bullet for himself.

Tony eventually returned from the war. He had been in town for less than 60 hours when he ran into an old acquaintance who stopped to talk to him. During the course of their conversation this guy told Tony that all Vietnam veterans were assholes. Tony couldn't believe his ears. He had just lived through a living hell and he had not received a welcome home, and no sense of gratitude, and this remark left him shocked. There was no respect for the Vietnam veteran. Many were referred to as baby killers and were spit on. He knew that California could be a hostile place for veterans, but he never dreamed that some of the people in his little hometown could be so cold. He was very surprised at the attitude of many of the American people. After that day Tony retreated into a shell and became a kind of loner.

"I remember walking down our driveway...I was in Marathon, Wisconsin...but I was still in Vietnam. I was scouting out the yard. I was not comfortable here in my own hometown in the United States. I no longer belonged here. Each night I was haunted by nightmares over and over again like an eight-track tape that kept playing over and over. Every night I was back in Gio Lihn. I would jump out of bed in a cold sweat and survived with very little sleep. Each morning I would go to work. I would work all day, come home and work on my tree farm until dark, shower, eat supper and fall into bed exhausted, only to relive those nightmares."

Tony's life became very dysfunctional. Besides being a loner, he was angry and had a very short fuse. He had no patience and said he was lucky that he wasn't fired from his job. He didn't care if he lived or died. Desert Storm and news from Iraq made him angry and triggered horrible nightmares. He didn't realize that the news, 1960s music, or the sound of a helicopter could be a trigger that would bring him right back to Vietnam. The squealing of car tires by local adolescents in town brought terror to him in the form of incoming rounds. There was no rest for him anywhere. The only time he felt he would be at peace would be when he was dead.

At age 55 Tony retired from his job. He couldn't go on any longer. He thought that when he retired, things would get better...but they only got worse. He was hurting and desperate when I first met him. Sleeping pills didn't affect him or help him to rest at night. He had a few close calls over the years with machinery where he had almost gotten severely injured. He had high blood pressure for several years, left untreated, in the hopes that it would eventually kill him. He contemplated suicide but his religion kept him from resorting to that. He knew he would go to hell, and hell was Gio Linh. And so he struggled each day for 30 years trying to find some peace and happiness. For 30 years he was extremely unhappy.

He came to meet us after being referred by a relative who knew about my husband's diagnosis and recognized some of the symptoms of PTSD. Tony drove 240 miles to our home to meet us. We talked for hours, and later that evening he and Ted attended a Vietnam support group meeting where Tony met other veterans who understood what he was living with. Someone else finally understood that night. Tony felt like he had finally come home. For the first time in his life he felt that there was hope. The veterans at that meeting helped him to unload some of his feelings and were able to give him their phone numbers so that he would have someone to talk to. They were able to direct him to a person near his own hometown who could help him to get therapy and someday recover or at least learn to deal with post-traumatic stress disorder.

There isn't necessarily a cure for PTSD. However, veterans like Tony are treated by being educated about the disorder and through therapy they learn coping mechanisms and learn what the things are that can trigger reactions in them. Eventually they find some peace and their lives become better. Tony has since received counseling and is on medication, which helps him to cope with his memories. He is very grateful for the help he received from the other veterans who understood and supported him during this time.

Gary

Gary and I graduated from high school in 1966. We were classmates for six years, middle school and high school, and although we were not close friends at the time, we had been in many classes together. From what I knew about Gary he was a very nice guy, never in any trouble. He was a very normal, well-adjusted person.

Gary

Gary was drafted at the age of 19. When he wrote to his parents just before returning to the states he said he was a changed man. His parents assumed that as a result of his service experience he had grown up. However, when he finally arrived at home they saw that he was a dramatically changed person. One they didn't know.

"I wanted to tell my parents that I loved them when I returned home, but I couldn't," Gary said. "I felt empty. I had no feelings. And I couldn't tell them."

His mother claims that he had many physical problems. He lost control of the use of his legs after the first two days at home. His temper was uncontrollable and he was easily upset. He didn't like being in crowds and couldn't stay in one place for very long. He was always complaining about one thing or another and he seemed to be very depressed. He was unable to sleep at night and was angry with the government. He had stomach problems and problems with his back, neck, legs and feet. Suffering with terrible night sweats and hurting both physically and emotionally, he was anything but the well-adjusted son she knew who liked school, sports and hunting and fishing as a boy.

Gary eventually reached out for medical help and was diagnosed in 1990 with PTSD. His therapist observed that he suffered from extreme agitation, lack of trust, fear of intimacy and closeness, memory loss, and a hypersensitive startle response. He felt a sense of helplessness and hopelessness and didn't feel that it was a situation he could recover from. He suffered from extreme isolation and had thoughts of suicide and homicide. He began to receive treatment and attended Vietnam veterans support group meetings. While applying for a disability, Gary couldn't concentrate and had a difficult time with all of the paperwork. During this time he went through a lot of emotional turmoil.

Gary was drafted and left Marquette on October 5, 1967, leaving on a Greyhound bus with 21 other guys. Even the ride to Milwaukee to the induction center was eventful. The bus kept stalling and they had to get out and push the bus a number of times. He eventually went to Ft. Campbell, Kentucky, for basic training. While he was in basic he became sick and was hospitalized with a temperature of 105 degrees Fahrenheit. As soon as his fever broke he was sent back to the bivouac area. Many young inductees suffered with upper respiratory infections due to a lack of sleep and a drastic change in climate. Most had to tough it out and get through the physical training, sick or not. If you went on sick call and missed much training you had to be recycled and go through it all again. The people from the north can't handle the cold humid clammy type of weather. They just can't acclimate themselves fast enough and so there are a lot of sick young men. They run you through the wet and the mud and the cold.

Gary also developed marching fractures in both feet. He was sent in for X-rays, and they applied casts to both feet. Later, due to worry that he wouldn't be able to take his final physical training tests, he tore off the casts and just barely made the mile run within the allotted time.

Gary recounts the following:

On October 1, 1969, I was flying, by way of Anchorage, Alaska, and Japan, to Bien Hoa, Vietnam. I was a clerk, Specialist 5. The first day I arrived in Vietnam I was taken to the 90th replacement center, in Long Binh, Vietnam. My first night I didn't sleep at all. We were told not to walk around after dark because they found one GI the previous night with his neck slit. Not having a weapon for protection, I picked the top bunk on the second floor. I watched spiders crawling on the ceiling and remember wondering if they were poisonous, as some were. I listened to the explosions all night long and could see skylight in the distance.

I spent 11 months and 21 days in Cam Rahn Bay, Vietnam, with the 59th Field Service Motor Pool. We weren't allowed to have our weapons. It was considered a secure area and so weapons were locked up in the armory. The only time I was issued my M-14 was when we were assigned to guard duty or when the sirens went off, letting us know that we were on alert status, or we were being rocketed by the enemy. When the alarm went off we would go to the armory, be issued our M-14s and would be loaded into trucks. We would be issued two clips of ammunition and were taken to different parts of the base to guard. On one occasion they gave me two empty clips and a total of three rounds and brought me to the only bridge that connected us to the mainland. On the mainland side we were the blocking force to watch guard.

At the bridge I was given an aerial flare and was told not to fire it unless I saw someone crossing the bay (like swimmers, or sappers as we called them, trying to blow up the bridge). I stayed there all night wondering what the three rounds were for; two rounds to warn the others and one round to shoot myself in the head if we were overrun.

I remember being assigned guard duty at the village as an E4, standing in the tower with only three rounds, watching the village with the bluff towering over me. I felt very vulnerable at these times, with only a field phone to call for help while being a perfect target for a sniper. The last time I pulled guard duty at the village I was a Spec. E5 and it was my 21st birthday. Another man and I had to man the phone lines to all the guard posts and ships and check on the posts from time to time by phone. We weren't given any weapons for protection. It was one of the longest nights of my life. We were worried about sappers or the VC walking in on us and not being able to defend ourselves. That evening when I took my sleep break I woke up completely soaked from head to toe with sweat, with red spots all over my stomach.

During one of our largest attacks I was sleeping. I was dreaming I was watching a 4th of July fireworks and suddenly woke up realizing that this was reality. We were being attacked. Everyone was running out of the barracks. Once outside, we started running into other company bunkers since we didn't have any (and still didn't have any when I left).

The constant worry and stress took its toll on Gary and he doesn't remember much about his last three months in Vietnam. He was in a continual state of anxiety and turned to drinking to help him survive the atmosphere and daily attacks. He believed that he wasn't going to go home anymore and wrote his last will and testament. As the time got closer to going home the more scared he got.

Gary made it home but had to have years of therapy and 35 years later still needs to take antidepressants, sleep, and stomach medications. He spends a lot of his time helping other veterans and working on his cottage in the woods.

Pete

It was the summer of 1967 and my girlfriend was pregnant. Our parents didn't know. I didn't have a job and tried to get into the Air Force but couldn't get in. I didn't want to be around during the holidays.

I knew I was going to be drafted in the near future. I was working at the post office and the Marine recruitment office just happened to be in the same building. One day a recruiter saw me at work and said he'd heard that I wanted to get into the service. He told me that two other guys from the area had signed up and were going to be leaving. I could go in with them. I went to take the test and later found out the other two guys had flunked. I would be going in alone.

The next thing I knew I was in the marines. In boot camp they wake you up in the middle of the night and make you run around. It is designed to push you to the limits, with the least amount of sleep, the maximum amount of exercise, all the while trying to teach you survival skills and to be the soldier who can take orders and carry them out to a high standard. I thought, "What the hell did I do now?" No matter what your military occupational specialty (MOS) ends up being you are trained to be an infantryman first. When I went on leave before going to Vietnam they said, "Don't get married when you get home because you're not coming home from Vietnam and your parents should get that $10,000 insurance policy. Your girlfriend just wants the money." I came home on leave and got married. My daughter was born in April of 1968.

I was a supply warehouse man in Vietnam. I worked on a big supply base north of Da Nang. We were hit nightly with rockets and mortars. One of my jobs was to go to the LZ (landing zone) and take body parts off of the trucks and put them on choppers. We were usually under fire, and my memories of this time were of blood, body parts, and screaming. I wasn't in the infantry, I was in the rear, on a base, but we still experienced constant mortar attacks. You never knew if it was the real thing or harassment.

In Vietnam we had to go up north, or on convoys to the shores of Da Nang, and pick up oil in these big tankers and ride back shotgun and they'd be shooting at us. I guess the worse thing was when soldiers would get hit with rockets and we'd have to sit and wait for the choppers to come in and we'd have to meet them and bring stretchers and get them off the helicopters. There were guys that had been shot and were screaming and trying to get off of the stretchers. I remember one guy getting hit with shrapnel and he was covered with a sheet that was just drenched with blood.

Before I left Vietnam I repeatedly went to sick bay and told them I didn't want to go back to the real world. Traveling home I felt out of place, scared and totally against society.

When I left Vietnam the plane landed in the middle of the night because they didn't want to deal with protestors. They told us, "We've got bunks but it's in the mental ward so if you are sleeping in a bunk above a patient be very quiet because he could wake up and kill you." That's the real truth. That's how we were greeted. Then they said, "If you go into San Francisco, into town on liberty, get civilian clothes from the PX." That's still in my mind. That was a low blow. Now, someone who wasn't in the service would think, Oh, they would never treat you like that.

When I returned to the states I didn't fit back into life, the way life was, and how it was for people who didn't go to Vietnam. Thirty years later I still don't feel like I fit in. When I returned people didn't know where I'd been, and when they found out they thought we were losers. No one knew what I had just gone through.

When I first got home I worked in the mine underground. I worked there for a year. I went to college and flunked out. I majored in accounting and I couldn't concentrate. I got a job in the post office and had a lot of problems. I was short tempered and had no patience. I had a lot of panic attacks and nightmares, and I'd see faces, and hear the cries and screams and rocket sounds in my dreams.

I'd go home at night and beat myself up because of the way I treated someone and I'd almost want to call them and apologize for the way I had behaved. I had to take medication and it would make me tired and some of the guys thought I was nuts and were wise asses and it was a lot of stress for me dealing with the public. I always thought I was just goofy. You can take a pill and you mellow out and have a nice day once in awhile but it's not going to erase everything in your mind.

I've had two marriages. The first one lasted thirteen years and the second one lasted a year. I've had two relationships that broke up, sometimes because they wanted to get married. At that time I wasn't ready for marriage.

Before I ever looked into getting help I knew there was something wrong with me. I'd see people that were so happy and I'd wonder how they could be that way. How could they look forward to another day? I never felt that way. I could never stay at home. I was in the bars and drinking all the time. My kids are 36 and 39 and I get along with them now but my kids went through a lot of hell. It was harder on them when I was living there with all the drinking and running around. My wife and I had problems and I was working long shifts. I didn't know what the heck was going on with me. My wife and I divorced.

I didn't trust people and kept relationships at arm's length. I feel a lot of anger and impatience. I've had ten jobs since I've been home. When I came home the only way I could function was if I was drinking or smoking pot and doing every other drug available. I didn't really know what was going on in my head. All I knew was that all I thought about was Nam and I wanted to get it out of my mind and so I would drink and take drugs to forget about it. I don't think I had any feelings. I didn't care about myself other than having a good time. I made a fool of myself all the time and made a lot of irrational decisions. Nothing made me happy. I had a plan that I was going to party until I died. I was going to get some cocaine, pot, scotch, Valium, and everything I could find. I had a large supply of Valium and so I planned to take the bottle and just go lie down.

In 1973 I attempted suicide. It was a nice summer night. I had the top down on my car and drove down this curvy road as fast as I could to the next town, which was about 20 miles away. I didn't care what happened…I just didn't give a shit. My intentions were to go. The Lord must have been looking after me because nothing happened to me and I didn't hurt anyone else. Now, I sit back sometimes and wonder how I ever got through it all. Not just Vietnam, but the time since I've been back. My parents told me later on that they knew something was very wrong. My dad is gone now but my mother is 84 and she has done a lot of reading about post-traumatic stress and watches everything on television. She knows a lot about PTSD now.

I started seeing a psychologist in 1977 in my hometown. I'd be in the medical center and I'd almost hide because I didn't want people to see me there, but I was doing something and my wife had told me, "You've got to do something." I finally went to Tomah Veterans Hospital in 2003 and it was a good program. The reason I went to Tomah was because I was working at the post office and I was going to hurt a supervisor...hurt him bad. I hated people of authority and being told what to do and when to do it. I had been having ghost nightmares where I'd wake up cold and sweating. Your mind doesn't let you know you're having a nightmare but your body knows and you wake up soaking wet.

While at Tomah the group therapy was good because you could talk with people who had been through it and would understand. I learned so many things while I was there. Many veterans are so impaired by the symptoms of PTSD that they are unable to function effectively or hold down a job. They are basically unemployable. I had so many jobs over the years. I cut hair, sold cars, did landscaping, worked at the power plant and the post office. I couldn't concentrate and I was impatient. It makes you feel awful when you do this in public.

I hope that by reading this book people will understand why we are the way we are. My long-term memory is good but my short-term memory is bad. I had actually been diagnosed with PTSD while I lived in Florida while attending a VA group but wasn't told. In 2002 when I sent for my records it said that I had been diagnosed in 1985. For 20 years my life was dysfunctional. At that time I was just divorced and I could have salvaged something if I had been told. There are so many veterans out there who don't know anything about this and they have short tempers and lots of problems but don't know anything about PTSD. Some are just too proud to go and get help. Talking with other veterans helps. Even today I have a hard time trusting people who are not veterans.

Pete has had extensive counseling and group therapy. The war haunts him and he lives with memories of his experiences. When asked how often he thinks about the war he said, "Mostly every day. Not always bad things, but how it's ruined my life." He feels that by becoming aware of the fact that he has PTSD, knowing its symptoms, and receiving counseling, his life has improved and relationships have been healing. "I believe in God," he said. "I believe that we have problems and that's the way life is, but I believe that God helps you get through these situations."

Pete, his therapist, and several other veterans recently made a video which appeared on the local public television station at our local university. He and the others want to help other veterans and make people aware of and understand what the country has put them through. "This idea of a white picket fence, a station wagon, three kids and a dog type of life is great, but most people who have not been in the military have no idea of what the people who protected the flag have had to go through. These poor guys coming home from Iraq are going to be worse off than us if they don't get help. Once PTSD is there, you're going to always have problems.

Recently Pete found someone to share his life with that he totally trusts. He feels that she understands him and PTSD. With their children, family and close friends standing by to support them, they got married this summer. It was so beautiful. As they danced to Natalie and Nat King Coles' song "Unforgettable," everyone was happy for them. It's been a long road for him and for everyone who cares for him. Now things are going well and hopefully he will have a happy, peace-filled life.

Glen

Glen served in Vietnam with the United States Marine Corps from September 1966 to September 1970. He was in Vietnam, in combat, from January 1969 to January 1970. He was a hydraulic helicopter mechanic and flew as a .50 caliber machine gunner on a Ch-46 helicopter.

"One of the most traumatic experiences was when we were picking up a recon team. The helicopter took fire from both sides and one engine got shot out. Just before crashing that engine started back up and we landed safely. I've had nightmares and flashbacks about dying. In my dreams I was reliving some of the times I got shot down in a helicopter. Why did the guys on the helo get shot and not me? I'd relive looking at a lot of wounded marines on medi-vac extractions under heavy fire. To this day the sound of a helicopter, or fireworks, brings me back to Vietnam. Watching TV War stories or Iraq on the news also brings back memories."

When Glen returned home he had a chip on his shoulder and wanted to be left alone. He just wanted to live a normal life. "Because of all of the anger, and the fights I got into when I came home, no one wanted to be around me. I was doing a lot of drinking and fighting at parties and in the bars. When I first came home my family was happy but eventually turned away (after a couple of years) because of my anger. I felt that I was okay and that the rest of the world was against me."

"I had many relationships but when I thought they were getting too close I would break up and find another. I didn't trust anyone and I lived in my own little world. I made a lot of irrational decisions. I was divorced once and remarried. I tried to bury Vietnam in a bottle of booze. I pictured myself as Ira Hays, 'The whiskey drinking Indian' that went to war. Over the years I've felt angry and impatient. I stayed drunk for 25 years so I wouldn't have to think about Vietnam. I used alcohol and drugs (speed and marijuana) to self-medicate. I got in trouble with the law. I was drunk and disorderly, arrested for spouse abuse and assault and battery. I didn't get along with my fellow workers and got layoffs without pay. I had to use up my vacation and sick time, and there was nothing left in the bank. I stayed isolated.

"I have three kids with three different women. My older boy went through hell, as did my step kids. My youngest daughter and I have a good relationship.

"Talking with other veterans helps me most of the time, but at times it's disturbing. I try to socialize with other people but it's hard for me to do. I feel like I'm on guard all the time. I attend counseling sessions and group therapy on a regular basis."

"L"

L served in the army in the Fourth Infantry Division from 1969 to 1970. His MOS was 11 B40—infantryman. He was married when he entered the service.

"L"

L saw a lot of injury and death while in Vietnam. As a result of his trauma he now takes antidepressants, antianxiety medication and sleeping pills. He has problems sleeping and suffers from night sweats and nightmares. Anxiety attacks and anger have gotten him into trouble since his return from Vietnam. He threw someone through a bar window while drinking heavily, and has been very combative and irritable. He has been described as a powder keg ready to explode. "You know, like when you're so angry you feel like you could kill someone?" he explains. "All of your feelings are bottled up and they come back to haunt you and affect the other aspects of your life, your marriage, your job, and your relationships with friends, family and coworkers." L worked on the railroad and in the school systems and PTSD has always affected his jobs. He finally had to quit.

His wife has stood by him and supported him and that is what has kept him going. When he was around his family he was okay, "but no one else wanted anything to do with me. I didn't feel like I fit in, but I didn't have an inkling that anything could be wrong with me. I thought it was everyone else. My old friends who were still in town when I returned from the war didn't understand and didn't really want to associate with me. They were still kids," he replies. "They had no idea of what I had just gone through. They had made judgments about Vietnam and had their own opinions about the war and the guys that went over there."

L had never worn his uniform in public on his leave home. Many people were against the United States' involvement in Vietnam and they didn't support the soldiers. "How could anyone talk about crawling across a field with machine guns firing over your head. Or having to kill another human being? I can still see their faces," he says. "One Halloween we were overrun by Viet Cong. They were inside the perimeter throwing cans of gasoline at us soldiers. It still haunts me."

The worst, most traumatic event he witnessed in Vietnam was when the guy sleeping next to him was attacked and eaten by a tiger. It still gives him nightmares. "I wake up at night and see a tiger in the hallway."

Talking about Vietnam helps, depending on who he is talking to. It's good to talk to another combat veteran because they are the ones who understand. Also, many of the young people nowadays have more respect for the Vietnam veteran.

Certain sounds and smells still bring him back to Vietnam. The smell of fires, the sound of a helicopter overhead, and hot humid weather affects his feelings and bring back memories. He loves to be alone, sitting in his garage, listening to music and loves to stand out in the rain. For some reason it makes him feel safe.

For some veterans, nighttime feels safe, while for others it doesn't. L's relationship with his wife is good but there was a time, when he met her in Hawaii on an R & R, that he felt like they were complete strangers. He had been in Vietnam for many months and was a changed man. When he first came home he drank excessively and made a lot of irrational decisions.

"I feel like I live in Vietnam every day of my life in many ways, but I have received counseling and have tried to help other veterans who are hurting and need help."

L has been very supportive of other veterans and helps them to get through the process of getting on the road to recovery.

J. P.

I was a fuel handler and also a grunt in Vietnam with the marines from June 1965 to June 1969.

J. P.

I was in boot camp in San Diego just three days after graduating from high school at the ripe old age of 18. After boot camp and infantry training, I went on leave and then reported back to Camp Pendleton for my orders—Vietnam. After all medical procedures were completed, we were flown to Okinawa; from there we boarded LSTs headed for Vietnam. Some marines were unloaded at Danang while the rest of us hit the beach in Chu Lai. Although it was supposed to be secure, we took mortar and rocket fire immediately—and we had no weapons or defense. I was scared as hell.

After being issued weapons and gear, we were sent to our assignments; it seemed like everyone was sent someplace different. Along with a few others, I was sent to Force Service Support Group Bravo. Another marine, L. G., and I decided we would like to be in action, so we volunteered to go to different combat units. One of the clerks covered for us while we were gone. This is how I ended up in combat, but our circumstances were unique because we could leave and go back to safety for a while before we went to other combat units. I have a great deal of guilt about this, wondering if I had stayed with one of these outfits I might have prevented some other marine's death. This has been very hard on me since I left Vietnam and remains with me to this day.

Nightmares started before I even left Vietnam. Within two days of returning home on leave my mother told me that I should get some help, that I was not the same anymore. I remember being afraid to come home because we heard other soldiers were being hit with paint and beat up. I did run into problems at O'Hare Airport in Chicago, but a police officer helped me out. I had an incident in my hometown bar. Three guys kept bothering me about the war. One of them pushed me, and that's all it took. I probably would have killed them if others hadn't held me off. One of the guys had to go to the hospital. After this I decided it was best not to let people know that I was a Vietnam vet. There were times when I said that I hadn't been in the military.

After leave I went to North Carolina where I finished my four-year hitch. I was assigned to the air wing at New River Air Station. I began drinking a lot, but one of the doctors intervened and convinced me to reduce my drinking significantly, but by now the nightmares and flashbacks started to be more frequent.

After leaving the service I was told by my mother after two days at home that I should get some help... that I was not the same anymore. I felt different, but I couldn't understand why. I didn't seek out people because I was learning that I was somehow different, and they only knew I was acting strange. I was able to function because I was in survival mode—I thought I could cope with anything. Little did I know! For a while I moved from job to job.

The drinking, nightmares, and flashbacks still haunted me. In 1971 I met my wife Judy and we were married in 1972. Without her I would not be here. She has put up with a tremendous amount of shit from me over the years. I did contribute to the raising of our two sons, but she was then and is now the backbone of our

Hope and healing with J. P. and his family.

family. The kids now understand why I acted the way I did and they are very supportive today.

About four years ago a couple of friends told me about getting help, that I had PTSD. I said, "Yeah, right!" After reading about the symptoms, I recognized myself. For a long time I thought I was going crazy. I remember being very scared when I started to get help. It brought everything back to the front and that was scary.

When I met Dan Forrester at Bell Behavioral and started to attend group sessions with other veterans, I realized I was not alone. Now we meet every Monday and try to figure out how to cope with everyday issues. These sessions have been a tremendous help.

The nightmares are not quite as bad now that I have some understanding of why. The intrusive thoughts still happen, but not as frequently. I think about Vietnam every single day since coming home—not a single day goes by that I don't think about it. Sometimes the thoughts aren't bad, but they are still there. I finally told my family about three years ago what I experienced in the war. I think they understand now.

I still feel like I don't fit in. I have a lot of feelings of mistrust. I became a workaholic until closer to the end. Now that I know I have PTSD I can look back and see that it had a lot of effect on my work and relationships with others.

What PTSD does to people is terrible. I've lost all the friends that I had before I went into the service, some through my choice and others by their choice. I still have a lot of guilt and anger to deal with and there has not been a day since I left Vietnam that I don't think about it. My friend L. G. is really a mess. I hope that some day he will get the help that he needs so desperately.

I wish that the federal government would have helped us out sooner; maybe that help could have saved the lives of so many veterans who have taken their own lives. And to the people that say, "Just get over it," I wish I could, but Vietnam will be with me forever.

Donny

I remember Donny as a teenager. He was probably about fourteen or fifteen years old and he was riding a beautiful horse through a field near my cousin's home. He was blonde and very good looking and seemed quite carefree at the time. Life later became very difficult for Don. Here's how Don tells it:

> I joined the Marines in September and six months later, on March 12, I was in Vietnam. I was sent to map and compass school in Da Nang. The Marines were on guard on the perimeter of that place. I was asked if I wanted to be the chaplain's assistant but I turned it down.
>
> I had graduated "honor man" at boot camp. The officers were drilling me with questions. "Why did you join?" I replied, "To fight for God and my country and fight for the people of South Vietnam."

During Don's tour of Vietnam he encountered many very traumatic experiences. He related some of the following to me one evening.

> In the middle of the night a helicopter dropped us right in the middle of a firefight. I didn't know where to go, what to do, or who was who. I got near an embankment and stayed there all night. There were dead bodies all over. When it was over I was asked to pray over the dead.

> We found an opening in the tree line. A guy stepped on a land mine. I held his hand while he was being patched up. We were human land mine detectors. We

were 12 miles South of Da Nang and they were all Viet Cong in that area. (There is a difference between the Vietnamese Army and the Viet Cong. The Viet Cong infiltrated into the general population.)

You'd get sniped at from villages when you were coming across and you couldn't see them. We'd end up calling in choppers and had to use smoke to give us a screen so we could get out of there.

During search and clear missions you weren't allowed to shoot unless shot at and couldn't destroy anything. After four months of getting shot at and not being able to retaliate we were told to search and destroy, and that's what we did. We made a village into a parking lot.

We had walked into an ambush. We were left there for 54 hours—two and a quarter days—and there was no one to help us. We had a chopper come in to get the wounded. Choppers resupplied us by dropping things from the air. After 54 hours the enemy left and we bandaged up everyone we could. We walked about a half mile so we could find a place where choppers could land. We had started out with 99 men. Eighty-eight were either dead or wounded. Eleven men were left, and I was one of them.

I remember running with these dead bodies to the helicopter. There was a pile of bodies six feet high. I remember running and falling on the pile of bodies.

I don't remember leaving Vietnam or how I got out of there.

I know that I was angry at God. I was angry at the politicians and the government. I was angry about a lot of things. I wanted to get everyone who was responsible for the Vietnam War. Before I had entered the marines I had spent a year in a seminary preparing to become a minister. I had signed up to serve my country because I felt that it was important. Fifteen years later I couldn't remember Vietnam. I had vague pictures in my mind but I really didn't know if they were real or on TV. I was attending an evangelism meeting in Tomah, Wisconsin, and I decided to go and meet an old childhood friend of mine who was a patient at the Tomah veterans hospital there. He had been diagnosed with PTSD. I met him and his wife there and went to a PTSD group session with them. As the first guy was talking I got a headache and my neck began to get stiff. I started to cry. The whole group was focusing on me. Things started coming back to me. I began sharing my story. I was sent to the head psychiatrist and he was trying to get me to stay at the hospital but I wanted to go home.

When I had returned home from Vietnam my survival was work. I would work until I dropped. I worked so hard I couldn't get out of the truck. Once I'd hit the pillow I'd sleep, but only for a few hours. I worked six days a week until 11 at night. I survived for 20 years doing that. One day I broke out in white bumps from head to toe and couldn't stop scratching. The only thing that would help me was a cold shower. I would wear socks on my hands so I wouldn't scratch. I went to the hospital and they gave me a shot. I fought the rash on and off for five years. It was almost constant for two years. The itch pushed me over the edge.

I was surviving with only two one-hour naps a day and would work all day. I began to see Asians in the woods in the middle of the day. They weren't the enemy. They had compassionate faces and they related to me. They were surrounding me. That really scared me. Until then I felt like I could survive and not need help from anyone. But it never came to be. I needed some help but didn't know where to go. Another veteran, a friend of mine, suggested that I see the psychologist that he was seeing. At that time I was thinking about taking myself out, and my wife with me. I spent a two-year period in my basement. I had dropped out of my support group. I was depressed and suffering from PTSD. I would sit and read stuff about PTSD and stories of other veterans.

I finally went to counseling, where I could put a name on what I was experiencing—post-traumatic stress disorder. It was a big relief. But even then I was a pretty sick cookie. I had a hard time going to counseling. I would drive there and sit in the parking lot and cry. The Doc would come out to the parking lot to get me. Afterwards I couldn't get home without crying. I had to stop on the side of the road. I was in counseling for three years.

Don continues to struggle everyday. His close relationship with other veterans helps him to regain his footing when he backslides. And in turn he helps other veterans at times when he is strong and they need reassurance and help. He was instrumental in getting a Vietnam veterans support group together years ago and has helped many other veterans seek help.

MARK

Mark was in the marines from 1963 to 1967 and in the reserves from 1974 to 1978. He was a recipient of the Navy Cross for Valor and the Purple Heart.

Mark met me for coffee at Wahlstroms, a cozy restaurant in Harvey. I was grateful for an opportunity to interview him. Mark, a very nice soft-spoken man, told me, "I was only 17, just a kid when I went into the marines. I joined because I was kicked out of the house. Of course I didn't think I was a kid at the time."

I did my basic training in San Diego, California. When you finally go to Vietnam you think nothing can happen to you. Then you begin to realize that it's real. If you can make it past the first few days you can make it.

Mark accepting the Navy Cross for extraordinary heroism.

On January 13, 1966 we were assigned to lead a patrol set up to help defend a platoon's position. We were moving the ambush to the secondary position and were moving down a well-worn path when I saw something white move to the side of the trail. It was so dark I had to strain to make it out. Suddenly two more bushes began to move. I yelled, "Oh God!" and began spraying the area to my left with my automatic. I noticed two mortars set up just off the trail and as many as 20 VC running up the hill, shooting down at the fire team. Our first thought was to keep the VC from taking those mortars, so we sprayed the area near the weapons with all we had. The retreating VC started showering us with grenades. We threw grenades back but two of them didn't go off. We were attacked by heavy automatic weapon fire. I was hit by a grenade and wounded but continued the pursuit and we secured the area. There were 30 of them and 4 of us. The next day we found that they had four 60 mm mortars, about 60 rounds of ammunition, two rifles and various items of field equipment.

I was patched up from my injury and returned to the field. When I got back to my squad, however, I was so jumpy that I was shooting at everything in sight, especially at night. The commanding officer said, "We need to get him out of here before he shoots one of us!" I had been through a lot for a 19 year old.

I've seen some awful things. My buddy was digging a hole and his shovel hit a land mine. His head was rolling down a hill. He was my buddy…and I was a mess.

I was a sniper and carried two rifles. One day we were walking down a trail. There were two small children playing, a boy and a girl. All of a sudden we saw two VC coming down the road towards us. They saw us and grabbed the children and held them in front of them like shields. We were trying to carefully aim for the VC and not hit the children, but one bullet grazed the little girl's head. We felt terrible. We got her to a hospital and she was okay.

When I came home to Flint, Michigan, the newspaper wrote up a big article about me. I started getting hate mail from all over the place and as far away as Ohio. I was called some pretty bad names. That was the single biggest impact. Then the VFW asked me to give a speech at their meeting. When I arrived I sat down with a group of people. There were World War II veterans and Korean veterans sitting at the table and none of them knew who I was or that I was the speaker. One of the guys said, "I don't know what this guy is going to talk about; Vietnam wasn't even a war." It made me sick to my stomach. I got up and left and didn't give the speech.

My close friends treated me all right but they thought it was funny that I was so jumpy and would throw firecrackers at me. I was jumpy and I'm still jumpy. It's a learned response. I began to keep to myself.

I built a log cabin out in the country. I had no neighbors. I just wanted to be left alone. I was isolated and drank heavily. I didn't deal with life well. I had three marriages. I was moody and would get into fights if you looked at me the wrong way. There was lots of anger in me. And when I drank it was like pouring gasoline on a fire. The anger exploded.

I had been so angry I didn't care about anything. I was driving 115 MPH and a cop stopped me. He said, "Look at those tires! They're bald! Don't you care if you get killed?" I was driving fast and reckless with bald tires and could have gotten killed but didn't care about anything. I had no reason for living. I finally joined AA and the anger subsided a lot when I quit drinking. I've

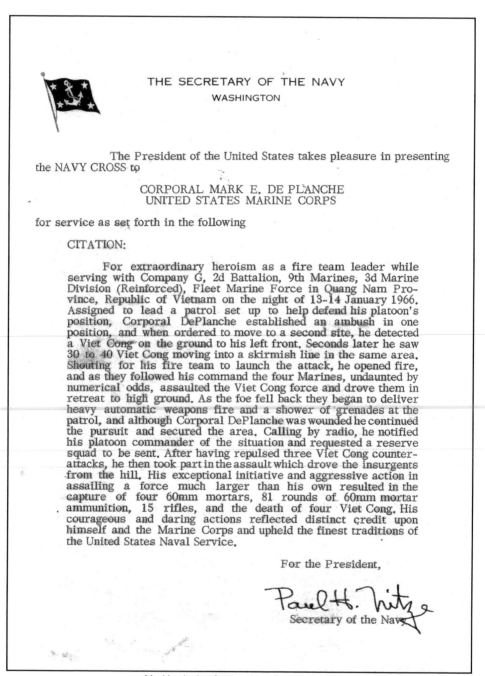

THE SECRETARY OF THE NAVY

WASHINGTON

The President of the United States takes pleasure in presenting the NAVY CROSS to

CORPORAL MARK E. DE PLANCHE
UNITED STATES MARINE CORPS

for service as set forth in the following

CITATION:

For extraordinary heroism as a fire team leader while serving with Company G, 2d Battalion, 9th Marines, 3d Marine Division (Reinforced), Fleet Marine Force in Quang Nam Province, Republic of Vietnam on the night of 13-14 January 1966. Assigned to lead a patrol set up to help defend his platoon's position, Corporal DePlanche established an ambush in one position, and when ordered to move to a second site, he detected a Viet Cong on the ground to his left front. Seconds later he saw 30 to 40 Viet Cong moving into a skirmish line in the same area. Shouting for his fire team to launch the attack, he opened fire, and as they followed his command the four Marines, undaunted by numerical odds, assaulted the Viet Cong force and drove them in retreat to high ground. As the foe fell back they began to deliver heavy automatic weapons fire and a shower of grenades at the patrol, and although Corporal DePlanche was wounded he continued the pursuit and secured the area. Calling by radio, he notified his platoon commander of the situation and requested a reserve squad to be sent. After having repulsed three Viet Cong counter-attacks, he then took part in the assault which drove the insurgents from the hill. His exceptional initiative and aggressive action in assailing a force much larger than his own resulted in the capture of four 60mm mortars, 81 rounds of 60mm mortar ammunition, 15 rifles, and the death of four Viet Cong. His courageous and daring actions reflected distinct credit upon himself and the Marine Corps and upheld the finest traditions of the United States Naval Service.

For the President,

Paul H. Nitze

Secretary of the Navy

Mark's citation for the Navy Cross medal

been clean and sober for 26 years.

While I was in Vietnam I was stationed in Da Nang for a month and one night when I was sleeping I felt something. It was a rat crawling on my chest. After I got out I remember my grandmother trying to wake me up and I swung at her and hit her. I felt so bad and apologized to her. I explained to her that if she was going to wake me up to say my name but not to touch me.

I can only sleep three or four hours a night. After about five nights I'm so exhausted that I will sleep about six hours. I tried sleeping pills and they had a bad effect on me. If I hear something at night I'm awake—there's no going back to sleep.

One day in AA I talked about living out in the country and wanting to be left alone. After the meeting a member came up to me and said, "You're a Vietnam vet, aren't you?" As we were leaving there was a loud bang and I really jumped. The guy said, "You need some help." I started going to a support group meeting with Vietnam veterans and they saved my life. It turned me into a person. When you go through the trauma of war you become an animal.

It's been forty years now and I'm still jumpy. My wife and I live near a lake and were out walking when I heard a noise—a duck quacked. I swung around with a stick in my hand like a weapon. My wife said, "What's that all about?"

Mark attends a woodworking class at the local university and seems to have normalized his life to a degree. He has developed some coping mechanisms that help him. But he has sacrificed a lot for his country and it has definitely taken its toll on his life.

Ron

Ron had thought long and hard about allowing me to interview him. It is hard for him to talk about things and said he wouldn't talk about war stories in Vietnam, but he would tell me about his life before and after he came from Vietnam.

I found Ron to be an intelligent, articulate and refreshing person. Talking with him brought back memories of my own childhood and the values I had learned growing up. Just by coincidence, since we grew up in the same town, I asked him if he knew my brother, Terry. He was a lot younger than Terry, but everyone seems to know my brother. He said yes, he did. In fact he considered him one of his mentors. "He was always nice to me and had helped me get my first job, washing cars, at a local service station owned by one of his friends."

Ron was born and raised in a little town in Michigan. He was born on April 13, 1949, and graduated from high school in 1967. He was confirmed at the Lutheran church. And so his story begins…

I was a hard worker when I was young. I had paper routes and would shovel sidewalks for the elderly on stormy days in the winter. They'd give me 50 or 75 cents and I enjoyed doing it. I was a happy person. I had good parents and grandparents. I had a very good upbringing. My parents made sure I had good moral teachers around me. Y'know in those days, kids were supposed to be seen and not heard. I was taught good manners and the golden rule; treat others the way you would want to be treated. I spent time with my grandparents who were of the Finnish heritage. My grandmother was a saint; she never said a bad word about anyone. My sister and I were treated like gold when we visited them.

I always did what I was expected to do and in the long run it was good for me. Like sometimes I would rather have gone rabbit hunting than Sunday school, but I didn't question it. I was expected to go and in the long run it was good for me.

I graduated from high school in 1967 and applied for a job in the mine. I went through the interview process and went for a physical and flunked the physical. I was told that I had a bad lower back and so they couldn't hire me. Those were the only good paying jobs in the area at that time. People either went to college or worked in the mines. My grandfather had worked there for 47 years and my dad worked there for 37 years and they had good work ethics and work records. I'd always thought I'd get my foot in the door, working a labor job and work my way up. But I flunked the physical. The only thing I could do was sign up for the service. I gotta have a job. So I joined the marines. My parents weren't too happy.

I was sent to the Marine Recruit Depot in San Diego, California, for 13 weeks of basic training, then to Camp Pendleton, California, to the Infantry Training Regiment. After that I was sent to Quantico, Virginia, Marine Corps Ordnance. I had 16 weeks of ordnance/ammunitions. I was trained to be a foreman overseer of munitions and explosives. After a 30-day leave, I went back to Camp Pendleton with the Ninth Marine Amphibious Brigade.

On September 13 I was given orders for Vietnam. When I arrived there I worked as an Ammo Tech (ammunitions technician) for Battery B-113.

It's been a long road for me...these experiences in Vietnam. I did what I felt I had to do and did it from my heart. I don't blame anyone. Because of my upbringing, if I did things for other people I always felt good.

I was stationed in the I Corps in an area called Red Beach. It was north and west of Da Nang approximately 40 miles. We were attached to the Second Marine

Twenty-Sixth Division. We were a mobile unit (105 Howitzer) and we came in on boats and made beach landings. One was a beach landing on Chu Lai. Our mobile unit was mostly in the north. Over there we didn't have the best of conditions. We slept on ammo boxes in the rain. My immediate supervisors were a lieutenant, a sergeant, and a company commander. I was in charge of all ammo storage, requisition, and proper handling of ammunition for each unit I was with. I was a corporal. It was a lot of responsibility that I had to learn in a real hurry. I was the only one and had to make sure that these things were done and done right. Daily I had to report to my company commander. It was a lot of responsibility for an 18-year-old kid from a small town where life was pretty innocent. There was no pressure those days in the small town I grew up in. I had a lot of pride in what I did and who I was and that's what forced me to do the things I had to do. All the things I did were survival techniques. The reason we went there was because of intelligence concerns of NVA (North Vietnamese Army) in that area. We were there to help protect civilian people in the villages—to help them so they didn't get killed.

I was there in Vietnam and I experienced what war was like. It wasn't a conflict. It was a war. We (the United States) were there for many years, thousands and thousands of Vietnamese people were killed and 50,000 Americans died. People were dying all around me. And it wasn't me. My time served in the military… well, I try to forget about it but I can't. I have a lot of feelings of anxiousness, guilt, and unworthiness. I have suicidal thoughts. I used to get in bar fights and have a lot of trouble with anger. I drank excessively and was arrested for drunk driving. Little things would set me off and I'd go and drink and it was always overdone. I couldn't just have a sociable drink. I'd drink too much and get into fights and in trouble with the police. I had lost my driver's license, my car insurance premiums went up and I caused a lot of problems for my family because of my stupidity. I wondered why I was doing it. After my second drunk driving charge my wife said she had it with my drinking and I should leave. When I was able to get help I could come back and see her. I know it wasn't a good environment for my sons. So I went to AA under court order. I stayed with my dad. I could see my kids anytime but I couldn't stay. I gave them all the money I had except for gas money to take care of my financial obligations. Finally, I was able to go back home. I didn't drink anymore (and haven't for years). I missed my family and they missed me. Drinking was my dark side. I have demons to fight but I also have angels around me to help me. After I quit drinking I lost a lot of friends, but I haven't drank for years.

Over the years I've had several jobs. I worked on construction, at a tire company, as a custodian at the university and then an old friend helped me get a job at the prison. The Academy of Corrections brought me back to basic training and boot camp. It was 16 weeks long. I worked in corrections for years. There were a lot of provoking instances at work. It was maximum security and housed the lowest of the lowest. They were life prisoners who had nothing to lose. And there are so many policies, procedures, and rules we needed to follow. People would get fired. If you were a minute late on your rounds and a prisoner hung himself you would get fired. That finished me. It was physically and emotionally exhausting. It drew the life out of me. This is all part of who I am.

I think cloudy sometimes and get moods. I mind my own business and go to see my kids and grandkids, but mostly I don't associate with people much.

Regarding Vietnam, I hid it. Swept it under the rug. It's an unacceptable thing to talk about. I was ridiculed at times and no one cared. (Now today veterans are being recognized.) A lot of what happened to me in Vietnam and things that happened there I've repressed. I've been diagnosed with post-traumatic stress disorder. I had such bad dreams that I tried to choke my wife. I felt hopeless and helpless and had low self-esteem. I also had thoughts of suicide.

I have lots of health problems. In 1990 I had a tumor in my neck that was diagnosed as non-Hodgkin's lymphoma. I have ulcerative colitis which is like a bad rash in my colon that bleeds. I've got heart problems and high blood pressure. I've had two angioplasties and have sleep apnea. A lot of my health problems came from stress. When I came home from the service I couldn't get a job in the mine because of my back. I have hearing loss and tinnitus from the loud bangs and shooting so I have to wear hearing aids.

In 1992 while working at the prison, I found out from an Agent Orange review that a friend gave to me that non-Hodgkin's lymphoma is caused by exposure to Agent Orange. I had been exposed. He suggested that I look into help from the VA…I went to see the VA representative for help and among some other information he gave me was a brochure to read on PTSD. I called him and told him I thought I had it. He told me to bring him my DD-214 and all the paperwork I had. All I had was a fire-watch ribbon—a good conduct medal. While in Vietnam my sergeant had called me down to his hooch. (Hooch is a plywood floor off the ground with a tent over it. It was his bunk and his office.) He said, "I have your orders to go home." He had my papers but didn't have papers for my medals. I could wait till he got them or I could leave. I chose to go home. But when I left he gave me a beautiful plaque. It said,

"For those uncompromising
Idealists
Who in battle chose the best in life
Knowing the best led to death.
Vietnam
Bastard Bravo
From the men of Bravo to (my name and #)"

After sending in all of my paperwork I received a 10% disability for the cancer, 10% for hearing loss, and 30% for PTSD.

My doctor in Milwaukee straightened out my meds, but if I take all my meds some days I wouldn't be able to function, so I take them as needed.

Now, back to work at the prison. I was having problems at work and wasn't functioning like I should, but I was hiding it. I don't like to make errors and other people depend upon me. I was under a lot of stress and worrying because of my job. I took a couple of stress leaves and did it under the recommendation of doctors. I tried to get long term disability (LTD) but was denied because it was service related. (If you served in Vietnam and have PTSD, insurance doesn't cover it.) I'm now without a job or insurance. I decided to tell them I wanted to retire. I have too many eggs in the frying pan. I've either gotta take 'em out or let 'em burn. I already have enough problems and now this is making it worse. This is a real problem. Then I got a letter from the State of Michigan Long Term Disability and it said that I could appeal it. It took me two days to write that letter defending myself. I stated, "I think the fact that I have to defend myself is belittling to me and downright discriminating." I don't think

I should have had to defend myself. I left because of the stress of my job and got a letter from the doctor. I got a letter saying I couldn't get disability because it was military related. I was mad, upset, and angry. This added more stress for me and my wife both mentally and financially...The appeal was denied. Now what was I gonna do?

My wife was badly injured in a car accident. She was in a trauma unit and very ill. I had no job and although I was covered by the VA, she had no insurance. The guy that had hit her had no job and had the nerve to drive a car that had no brakes and no insurance. I called my insurance agent who gave me a number to call downstate. I had to talk to a machine. Five days later there was no response. I hadn't made a claim in 18 years. I went to a lawyer and told him the predicament I was in. He would help me but I had to pay a $1,000. That was a year ago and I haven't gotten anything. My wife isn't well, always in pain, and I've had to take time off of work to take care of her. I went to the social security office to apply for disability and showed them all of my doctor's reports. I was denied. I needed money so I had to cash in my 401K (the prison system doesn't have a retirement, they have a 401K). I've tried to get the records of the medals I was given because I needed that to get help. I wasn't able to get those. I'm not looking for a handout, just what is coming to me so I can make ends meet. I think an illegal alien could get more assistance than I can. And I served my country.

Finally I got in touch with an old buddy of mine from the marines. He and I went through a lot of training together and I ran into him in Vietnam. We were both riding in trucks and noticed each other. We had become best friends and had called each other moon face because we both had a round face. It was great to see him. I told the driver to hit the brakes because I thought I saw someone I knew, and he had done the same thing. In basic we used to argue about whether or not there was a God. He was an atheist and I wasn't. He had been a supervisor, a sergeant who worked for a headquarters's battalion overseeing things. Years later when I talked with him I explained what was happening and how I needed help. He wrote a wonderful letter for me verifying my record in the service to help me get some more compensation from the VA. Besides a wonderful letter and a great conversation, I learned that after all of those arguments about whether or not there was a God, he had become a minister!

Telling my story has been hard but I have to do this. But I feel it's an honor to do it. I hope that someone will benefit from my experience.

Ron learned one important thing as he went through the process of seeking help. Sometimes, if you aren't able to get the correct information that the VA needs you can ask people that you know from the service to verify it for you on paper.

PETER

Pete is a kind, nonviolent, peace-loving person and a close friend. He went through basic training at Fort Campbell, Kentucky, infantry at Tigerland in Fort Polk, Louisiana, came home for a month, and flew across the pond to Cam Ranh Bay, Vietnam.

I was then sent to Tan son nhut to the 101st Airborne Division. The first night there they got shelled. Of course there were ditches outside. While there we slept on wire cots and a mattress—no sheets.

Then I went to Phu bai, which is in the mountains, 50 miles away from Da Nang.

In the Au Sha Valley we had a few helicopter assaults. The forest canopy was so thick you couldn't see anything in the daytime. You didn't know if you were getting into something. I was in country for about one month when we (a small patrol) were sent to a river. Most of the guys were going to swim in the river but I was real tired and went to sleep. When I woke up no one was there. They had left me there. I had to find my way back to the perimeter. I was singing my way back so I wouldn't get shot!

At one point during the bad weather season there were about 100 of us caught in a typhoon. It was wet, windy and rainy and we all sat hanging on to one another's ruck sacks. There were lots of bomb craters around us with pools of water but not much food. I remember trading my jelly for cigarettes. We didn't have many supplies and were wet for three or four days. (We couldn't change clothes for a month.)

There were lots of patrols and ambushes. We had to climb the mountain and climb back down again. It didn't make much sense. I guess it was to acclimatize us. After about six months our whole unit was sent south to a place outside Saigon to protect air force personnel (so they could sleep in their beds and eat their steak every night). We were on the outside looking in.

We were into firefights to support Bravo Company. It was the first time I saw a dead NVA. Everyone is just shooting at each other. Geez! When you see someone with blood bubbling out of him up close you wonder if he had a family. It turned me against war…You'd find guys on the trail all mashed up, but you don't ever talk about those things.

I got out of the field early. After ten months in I signed up for the helicopters. I had to get out of the field. I went out for a month and when I came back the first thing they told me was to build a hooch door in the rear for a few pets. I said, "I couldn't do that, I'm in transit. I'm not going to do that." The officer in charge got mad and said, "Are you refusing a direct order?" I really didn't have much respect for him, he was just putting in time. Well, I ended up building the hooch door anyway.

We spent some time in the mountain yard area. The mountain yard people were hunters. They were a little different than the Vietnamese people, and looked more Polynesian, with round eyes. They were quite unique, and carried bows and arrows. They were a primitive tribal people who lived totally off of the land. They would clear areas of the dense forest and farm those clearings. They used oxen or water buffalo to accomplish the hard work. They built their huts made of sticks and straw about four feet off of the ground. They were a peaceful people. The NVA used to impose themselves on them, take their food, and holed up in those mountain yard villages. Whenever we encountered a mountain yard village we would surround it, then sift through it looking for NVA holdouts. When the soil was depleted in one village they would move to another new area and make a new village with good farmland (soil) that could support them again. The villages were always on the move. The Vietnamese didn't like them and it's said that they drove them to that type of existence. They lived in tough areas in the Chuprong Mountains where all the dangerous animals, such as tigers, panthers, elephants, lived.

As a helicopter gunner we were in hot LZs quite a few times and lost crews. We'd get hit once in awhile but we also had a lot of mechanical troubles. We were often in WWII helicopters that had been patched up. We would be firing on people you never saw and you never saw the result. I guess it kept your sanity.

I was a door gunner on a Chinook helicopter, a big troop carrier. It had a big blade on the front and on the back. We were steadily on the move. We would bring troops and supplies and get medivacs out of the field. At this particular time, we hooked on to two large rubber blivets filled with fuel and were going to transport them to a different area. A man would stand underneath and hook on to the blivet and the helicopter would move forward and would be hooked on to the second blivet. Then the helicopter would leave. On this day, there was a platoon of troops (30) inside and two rubber fuel blivets. When they went up a few hundred feet the Chinook lost power and started coming down. (My first thought was, "There goes my R & R!")

I figured I would jump out of the gunner window, but I was afraid that when the helicopter hit ground the blivet would blow up. But instead, the rubber cushioned the fall, and luckily the fuel didn't explode. As the helicopter crashed the blades continued to turn and also kept going up and down. I landed on the ground, bruising my body, blackening my eyes, and injuring my ankles and back. I was lucky; many weren't. The blades of the Chinook went through the fuselage (the body of the aircraft) and cut the troops in half.

This isn't something you talk about. You just as soon forget it. There were times when you would see bodies thrown in a heap. You don't know who's under that plastic, whether it's friend or foe, and it's good you don't know.

When we left Vietnam we were told not to wear uniforms to go back home. We were aware of the bad feeling against the war and were told to be as "non-military" as possible. When I first got home there was a sense of euphoria. You couldn't believe you were home, this couldn't be. I immediately left for Detroit to visit my brother John and to pick up a new car. I drove it through Chicago and back home to Marquette.

How did the war affect me? Over the years I worked constantly, 24/7. I kept very busy. I suppressed intrusive thoughts by working. I had a job where I could throw myself into it. I had computers at home and would work all day, at night, and on weekends. At the end I burned myself out. I didn't trust my own work and would go over and over it, double-checking everything.

I don't really get close to anybody. If something happens people get hurt all over again. I'd have a kind of comradeship with people who went through the same experiences, but you become a loner. I'd just as soon be alone as with others. I'm quiet and my wife says, "Talk! Aren't you happy?"

At night I was always dreaming, looking for my rifle, and then I'd be looking for ammunition. In my dreams I kept getting drafted and I would say, "I've already been there!" Once in awhile you see something that brings you back to Vietnam and then you'll dream about it at night...

A starlight is a nightscope, and at night we would watch the rice paddies with the starlight, because we saw movement there earlier. Three or four hours into the night the VC walked right into the perimeter. There was lots of fire and action but no one got hit.

They ran right through the other side of the perimeter. I said, "Good, no one got hurt!" It was a thankful day. No one got hurt, not even the enemy.

Most of the time when we were out in the field, many days would go by without seeing anything. You're always waiting for a quiet day.

D. W.

I was in the army from July 1968 to September 1969. I was trained as a mechanic and ran a big towing wrecker with a crane boom. We went to firebases to repair machinery. We would replace blades on helicopters. We were on the road most of the time. We didn't spend much time in a shop. There was a lot of danger on the road and only two guys on a truck. There were mortars and rockets all the time. We went on surprise inspections on the firebase where there was artillery.

After a couple of weeks in Vietnam I was hitchhiking. A truck picked me up and gave me a ride. I was going to a small BX and we came under rocket attack. There were rockets everywhere and there was nowhere to go. I was running, trying to run for a ditch, but I was caught out in the open with nowhere to go.

The base camps were bigger targets and rocket attacks were around you every day. I didn't get much sleep, maybe two or three hours a night. When you would hear rockets at night you would wonder if it was incoming or outgoing and you couldn't get back to sleep. You'd listen awhile because you could tell by the sound. When the B-52s would start bombing it was like raining bombs and the ground would shake so bad that the metal Quonset huts rattled like a tin shack in an earthquake.

I was up north, south of the DMZ (demilitarized zone), a short way off the Ho Chi Min trail. They were bombing constantly along that trail. The marines were below us, in the foothills of the mountains. Their shells would hit our area. I spent the Tet offensive north near the DMZ, and after the Tet offensive we were sent down south to reinforce the Cambodian border.

During my tour of Vietnam you couldn't trust anyone. Children even carried grenades. A bunch of kids would run up to the truck asking for candy and one of them would put a grenade in the gas tank. You had to be careful and watch everyone.

In a letter to the Department of Veterans' Affairs, D. W. explains how the war has affected his life. He has been diagnosed with PTSD with a 30% disability but feels that his evaluation was brief and minimized the effects of PTSD that he was suffering from. He says:

My disability began in 1992. The doctor reported in my evaluation that I have never had suicidal thoughts. However, this is not true. I told him that I do have suicidal thoughts, and I specifically told him about these feelings.

I tried to tell the doctor about the time I came very close to committing suicide…but he cut me off and would not let me finish what I was saying. It was the fear of committing suicide that finally got me to seek help for PTSD.

In regards to my work record, the doctor's report states that I have "maintained employment over the years." The truth is I was able to work as a pipe fitter for 19 years of which the last six were as a service representative. I haven't been able to work since the age of 44. After my discharge from the military, I worked for more than 20 employers. I was never able to maintain steady employment with an employer for very long. Some told me I had a bad attitude, or that I wasn't a team player. There was always some reason that I was being laid off. The longest I held a job was the last six years as a service rep. There I worked by myself and my employer was from out of state and I hardly ever saw my boss or anyone else from the company. My interaction with my employer was basically by mail and telephone. The distance between us was the buffer zone that I needed.

My evaluation with this doctor was very brief, lasting less than an hour. It consisted mostly of answering questions from a checklist with yes or no answers. I wasn't given time to elaborate on my answers. When I did try to elaborate, he gave me the impression that he wasn't interested, and seemed to cut me off and go on to the next question. It is hard for me to understand how anyone could get a real feel for what the effects of PTSD have had on my life for the last 40 years in less than an hour. I have been in counseling for just over a year and I am still learning the effects it has had on me. Things that have happened that I had not even considered as part of PTSD have been brought out. I have had problems trusting others, especially the government. I lose my temper over little things. I have guilt feelings, anxiety issues, and flashbacks. Now I have found out that these are all part of my post-traumatic stress disorder. These symptoms have been a part of my life for 40 years and I feel they were minimized in the doctor's evaluation.

After serving in Vietnam, I have always had a problem getting a night of restful sleep. For the first four or five years I drank to excess which seemed to help with sleep. After having problems due to drinking, such as marital problems, doing stupid things such as driving drunk, having suicidal thoughts, and being more apt to act on them, as well as being sick all the time, I decided to give up drinking to excess. I was again having trouble sleeping. I found that working long hours helped me sleep so I began working long hours. I would come home from my regular job and work on my own projects. After working for eight hours, I would work another eight hours at home.

Over the years, I set up a mobile home, built an addition on it, built my own septic system, drilled my own well, did all of my own plumbing and electrical work and then did all my own landscaping and built a garage. I then started building another house and a garage. I worked nearly everyday for 13 years until it was done, all of it by myself. During those years I also repaired my own vehicles, appliances, and anything that needed to be fixed. I seldom took vacations or weekends off. All I did for years was work. This helped me to sleep but it brought on other problems. My wife always complained about being ignored, about my inability to communicate, and not having an emotional bond with her, and she divorced me.

I continued to work like a madman as it kept me from dwelling on the past, kept the intrusive thoughts at bay, and kept me from getting depressed. It helped me to sleep. In 1985 I went to work for a company as a service representative for heating and air conditioning controls. I serviced commercial buildings such as schools, hospitals, and other large buildings. I was able to learn my job but it required working long hours, many that I donated, or was not paid for. I did it because I liked the job and it allowed me to work alone, which I liked.

After about four years the long hours began to catch up with me and I started to feel run down all the time and had trouble with sleep. I started having pains in my back and neck, and headaches. I was having problems with clumsiness and concentration. I found myself making mistakes at work and had several job-related injuries. I fell from a ladder injuring my knee, which required surgery, and had several back injuries. I had so many in fact, that my employer sent me to a clinic for a "fitness for duty" evaluation. This caused me a lot of anxiety because I really liked the job and I felt that they were looking for a reason to fire me.

My bouts of depression were becoming more numerous and lasting longer. My problems at work kept getting worse and my pain became worse. I was really having a lot of problems with concentration and memory on the job and was becoming a danger to myself and others. I shorted out a 449-volt control in a panel, burning the shaft off of my screwdriver a foot from my face, spraying molten metal into my forehead and ruining my glasses. Another time I wired a boiler control wrong in an elementary school and thought about it when I was 50 miles away. I returned to find that I had done it wrong, which could have caused the boiler to explode. These are just a few examples. I would fall asleep while driving to work in the morning, fortunately waking up in time to gain control of the car.

All of these incidents were totally out of character for me as I have always been a fanatic for doing things right and double checking my work. I started to lose confidence in myself and my ability and was constantly second guessing myself. I started to feel like I was going crazy. I would make a mistake, get frustrated, and then make more mistakes. My problems seemed to be compounded and the frustration I felt was unbearable. Because of the headaches, confusion, and memory loss, I thought I might have a brain tumor. My productivity was suffering and my employer was asking why my jobs were taking so long. I tried making up for my mistakes by working longer hours and not putting them on my time sheet. When I screwed something up I would replace them with my own money so my employer wouldn't find out. I worried about having to lie to my boss to cover up for my mistakes.

I began to have trouble with irritable bowel syndrome and pain on one side of my face. The pain would last for about three days and then subside, leaving my face feeling numb. About a month later the pain would start again. It was a very extreme pain, so bad that I could not even wear a hat. I had gastroesophageal reflux disease and had a total loss of libido. I was sick with colds or the flu much of the time. My depression was getting worse. It seemed like my life was in a downward spiral. Since my doctors didn't seem to have any answers and physical therapy wasn't helping, I decided to make an appointment at the Mayo Clinic. I fully expected them to tell me that I had a brain tumor or something of that nature and that I only had a short time to live. By that time I didn't care if I lived or died. They told me that I had indeterminate myofacial pain syndrome and that there was no cure for it, but I wouldn't die from it. They also found that I had osteoporosis. I was very disappointed that they had nothing to offer me other than a diagnosis. I felt like I would be better off dead than the way I was. Suicide started to feel like a more viable option. One of the doctors that I saw at the Mayo Clinic advised me to make an appointment with the VA when I got back home. I tried to make one but was told that I was not eligible. I cannot remember the reason why.

I told my employer I would need to take some time off to get my life back together. I lost faith in the medical profession and felt like I was better off not telling the doctors everything about me after some insinuated that I was a hypochondriac. After six months I hadn't gotten any better so I applied for social security disability. After two years I started to feel somewhat better. I made a lot of lifestyle changes and was able to get along on 25% of what I had been earning when I was working. I continued to have most of the symptoms but at a more tolerable degree of severity. I tried to keep busy with small projects like gardening and other low stress activity. I realized that stress exacerbated my symptoms so I tried to stay low-keyed as much as possible. I would isolate myself and only deal with other people when there were no other options. I stopped going to church and didn't participate in any of the organizations that I had belonged to. Even family gatherings, especially funerals, were hard for me and would cause undue stress.

I was getting by until the war in Iraq and Afghanistan started. I began to have more nightmares and depression. Many of my other symptoms got worse. I could hardly make it through the nightly news on TV without crying. I started feeling just like I had before I quit working.

During a routine revisit at the local VA clinic, while talking to the doctor, I was having a hard time holding back the tears and he must have realized that I had a problem. We had a long talk and he suggested that I get evaluated for post-traumatic stress disorder. I was reluctant because I knew very little about PTSD. I knew I had a problem but I didn't think it was PTSD, so I said I'd think about it. I got some information on it and found that I had many of the symptoms.

I was still reluctant to accept counseling. I thought that I could handle it myself and I worried about what other people would think of me if they knew that I had this type of problem. (PTSD is a severe stress reaction.) Six months later I agreed to an evaluation. I now realize that PTSD and depression were the cause of my sleep and memory problems, which led to, or exacerbated, the other problems. However, at that time I didn't know about PTSD or what it was.

I continue to have problems with all of the issues I've stated except for the facial pain. I continue to have numbness in my face. I have lost the capacity to earn a living, lost most of my friends, and lost the majority of my pension. I have a broken marriage and happiness has eluded me for what seems like my entire life. This seems like a high price to pay for serving my country.

This veteran not only had the typical emotional and psychological symptoms of PTSD, but he also had many physical medical problems which were all connected to PTSD. A lot of the veterans I spoke with in my interviews suffered from osteoporosis, thyroid problems, irritable bowel syndrome, diabetes, and fibromyalgia.

D. W., like many other veterans suffering from PTSD, has a hard time sleeping. According to scientists, the role of dreams is to combine the stressful, or threatening experiences we have, with past memories in order to expand the brain's storehouse of survival capabilities. As the veteran dreams, these memories set off a kind of muscle bracing (relating to a traumatic experience) which reenacts whatever the body did in the traumatic experience. Blood vessels constrict and dilate, which leads to awakening with pain. The interruption of our dreams cause us to awaken before the dream is complete—the person becomes dream deprived—and it causes fatigue, irritability, and emotional and cognitive impairment. This cycle has been proven in fibromyalgia patients through the use of electroencephalograms.

Al

As Al walked into my kitchen, we met for the first time. I felt very comfortable talking with him as he was a very warm, sincere man. He began our conversation by telling me that by having PTSD he had gotten himself into a lot of trouble because of his impatience and a short fuse.

Many of the veterans I interviewed said that they had short fuses and had acted in an inappropriate manner due to a lack of patience and a constant feeling of anger beneath the surface. They didn't seem to care what other people thought of their actions or behavior. Al was no exception.

My brother Mike had been in Vietnam from 1967 to 1968. He'd been on the Delta on the riverboats. I flew out of Marquette, Michigan, for Vietnam one hour before my brother, Mike, landed there, returning from Vietnam. While Mike was there he was hit in the back and his friend Jimmy, from Ishpeming, dragged him out, loaded him on a chopper and saved his life. They were friends and had gone through boot camp, advanced infantry training, and Vietnam together, which is very unusual. They also came home together that day. Mike was very much affected by the war. He became an alcoholic and lived in the basement of my mother's house. He was very reclusive and wasn't able to handle things like family gatherings, or even more than two people at a time. Nothing could help him.

Mike's Obituary

Michael, age 59, died Thursday, June 15, 2006, at Bell Memorial Hospital where he had been a patient for four days.

Michael was born in Ishpeming on April 22, 1947. He was a member of the Catholic Church and Vietnam Veterans of America Chapter 380.

Mike was a Vietnam veteran from 1967-1968 in the 4th of the 47th Ninth Infantry Division. He was awarded the National Defense Service Medal, Sharpshooter, Expert 2 o/s Bars, Vietnam Service Medal with two Bronze Stars, Vietnam Campaign Medal with Device 1960, Purple Heart, Combat Infantry Badge and Army Commendation Medal for his bravery and outstanding service. Vietnam made him a decorated hero, but it also gave him a troubled soul. Being a sensitive person, he struggled with the aftermath of the war the rest of his life. Mike fought a brave battle in Vietnam and also at home. He will always be a hero.

My brother Mike and I were both in the army, the Ninth Infantry Division. I served from 1968 to 1969. When I got on the plane we flew from the West Coast to Alaska, then to Japan and Vietnam. When we landed in Vietnam, of course, I felt very apprehensive. The first person I laid eyes on when I got off the plane was a guy from my hometown. He was a truck driver and I recognized him right away.

They brought us out to the field, to a hooch. I was kind of caught off guard. There were three guys there who were all messed up with drugs. I didn't expect that. I kept thinking, "Holy Christ, is this what happens to these guys over here?" That was my first experience.

I was assigned to Charlie Company. I put in lots of chopper time. We'd get picked up and dropped off. I had 100 hours of flying time in hostile areas. There were nine holes in the helicopter. You'd sit on your helmet so you wouldn't get shot in the ass.

I was there during the Tet Offensive, an all out effort by North Vietnam to attack any firebases or main bases. They hit anywhere they possibly could—human wave attacks, to take American bases and try to win sectors of South Vietnam. They were repelled back after many weeks of fighting, but there were tremendous casualties on both sides. A lot of places the Americans were caught off guard. Everyone was being hit at once and so no one was there to help out. In 1969 they were still talking about it.

My company was rebuilt twice while I was there because of casualties and normal rotation. We walked through booby-trapped areas almost every day. Every time we walked in we'd lose a couple of guys. When we walked through booby-trapped areas it was very intense. You had to almost memorize where each guy put his foot. It took us five hours to walk 30 yards.

There was a guy named Rabbit from Pennsylvania. He had two Purple Hearts. I remember he was sitting on a bunker and he had a picture of his wife and baby on the stock of his rifle. His wife was expecting another baby. The guy was real emotional and depressed. He said, "I'm not afraid to die, but I know I won't live to see my baby." It was a kind of premonition because that day he went out and took a direct hit and was killed.

Another guy I knew had gotten wounded twice and he was getting short— his time remaining in Vietnam was short and he would be going home soon. He had a good friend who did him a favor. He made a slice in his foot so the guy wouldn't have to go back out into the field again. Remember, he was getting short and had two Purple Hearts already. His foot was starting to heal and he would have had to go back out into the field again. I looked at his foot and quickly ripped his foot open again so he wouldn't have to go back out. You were the most vulnerable the first couple of months you were in Vietnam and the last couple of months, when you were short.

On my first mission out in Vietnam we hit a gook. We trailed him like a deer, following blood. We finally caught up with him and he'd been hit in the lung. The medic was checking him and as he turned him over you could hear the kid gurgle and die. The gooks usually hid their bodies. They yanked them down into holes and hid them.

We had to follow orders. Sometimes we'd be in a no-fire zone. There was a batch of North Vietnamese and we couldn't shoot at them.

We found a medical cache. It was a crock, buried under the ground, and it was a quick set up Vietnamese medical hospital. (We found a gold plated needle syringe which I saved. The North Vietnamese would reuse them.) We ended up staying there for three days. We didn't have water and so I drank water out of the rice paddy and got malaria. It was 100 degrees out and I was freezing. I had two blankets on me and I was sweating and shaking like a leaf. I walked five clicks (5,000 meters) to a firebase with malaria. I could've had a chopper take me in but there were guys worse off than me and I figured the choppers were needed.

One day we were walking along a river. There were a lot of canals that irrigate the Mekong Delta. We were getting beat up pretty bad and were losing guys, so we were sharing platoons. I was at the tail end of my platoon. There were bunkers along the river, which we were blowing up so that if anyone was in the bunkers they wouldn't get behind us. The process was slow. So they had set up a booby-trap ahead of us. The tide in the river goes up and down and I thought it was odd that I saw a piece of wire sticking up out of the ground. I looked at it, and just as I was thinking, I heard a boom. A couple of guys were wounded, and right away I knew what it was. I ran up to the commanding officer who was hollering, "Incoming!" I said, "No, its not incoming, its command detonated." This meant that it was set so that when the first one went off and everyone hit the ground, they would get hit on ground level. I was standing up and didn't have a scratch on me. Everyone around me was hollering, and then we had to deal with a firefight from across the river! There were only a handful of us, six or seven guys left, that weren't hurt. I was hauling guys around the bunker and behind the bunker. There were all kinds of banana trees and we had to make a clearing and chop a bunch of trees down so the chopper could get in to take out the injured. It took a long time to get everyone on choppers.

There was one thing that really bothered me. There were a lot of guys injured, but there was this one guy who was whining and really crying. He wasn't hurt that bad and there were other guys with holes in their back the size of my fist, both legs broken, and scalps pulled back. They were really in bad shape. My platoon sergeant was lying dead in the water. The guy who was whining was jeopardizing other lives and so I walked up to him and slapped him and told him to shut up…

That really bothered me. I don't really like to talk about this. It really bothers me. But if this book helps someone else…

We had to carry extra weapons and duffle bags back to base camp that they couldn't take on the choppers.

One night we were pinned down in a rice paddy dike. I fell asleep and when I woke up there was a rat sleeping on my belly. I suppose it was warm. At night we were always soaking wet. There were lots of canals. I had elephant foot three times and ringworm was a constant battle. There were these guys we called shammers. They'd try anything to stay out of the field. One guy was on bunker guard and had ringworm. He kept rubbing it and scratching it so he wouldn't have to go out into the field.

While I was in Vietnam I broke my shoulder once, and I ran into some boards or something one night and hit my head and wrecked my neck, but I came out of it pretty good.

During the rainy season it was so wet that it was like loon shit and there were mud slides. During the wet season you'd take a step and there was so much mud you had to actually pull your foot out. It just kind of sucked your foot down.

When I came home from Vietnam I drew unemployment and started partying. The guys from Vietnam didn't talk much and most people didn't want to hear about it. I partied from 1970 to 1971. In 1971 I got married. I was married for ten years and then got divorced. I have three boys. I can't control myself at times and I have no patience. No one understands why you act the way you do. I've been fired twice. The second time was when I called the boss a scumbag and told him he'd turn his mother in for a quarter. I was arrested for felonious assault because a guy called me a scumbag and I let him have it.

I've been having bad dreams lately. I used to smoke pot and I'd wake up soaking wet and shaking, but I didn't remember the dreams. Now I don't smoke pot anymore and I'm dreaming a lot. Sometimes Vietnam seems like a dream. Some veterans become emotionally imbalanced. Emotional attacks come out of nowhere. All of a sudden you're in tears. It's really frustrating. Some guys see PTSD as a sign of weakness, but I'm an ass kicker. It was survival.

Why did I go for help? I had just been fired from my job and didn't have any insurance. I had hurt my hand and went to the drug store and got some stuff to patch it up. A friend of mine saw me there and talked me into going to the VA for medical help. I was so pissed off at the time. I walked into the VA clinic and fell apart. I started crying and just fell apart. I was told that I had problems, post-traumatic stress disorder. I had no idea. You know you can look out, but you can't see in. I had no idea. That's when I finally got some help.

Al is on medication and has been going for counseling. He helped to make a PBS program about PTSD, along with his counselor and other veterans. "I want people to realize how some veterans suffer for the rest of their lives. The emotional pain and stressors from time spent in the war affect you for the rest of your life. I want people to know how lonesome we are. Veterans have a lonely feeling in them and it doesn't want to go away. You want to self-destruct. We get fed up, and the hell with it, you can only take so much. As I got older it got worse. It's so late in the game, it's been too long and it festers. It turns into a permanent problem."

I suppose your impression of him might differ depending upon whom you were talking to because of the explosive nature that occasionally surfaces. For example, he began to tell me the story of how he was taking care of his brother's dog for a period of time. His brother had never taught the dog anything, and the dog barely knew his own name. Over a period of time Al was losing patience because the dog would not come, or listen, or obey any commands. One day the dog got loose and ran off. Al had to chase the dog all over the neighborhood. By the time he finally caught up with him he was exhausted and his fuse had run out long ago. "I wasn't hitting the dog, or hurting him, but I was mad and hollering at him. As I walked back towards my house, screaming at the dog, my neighbor lady came outside and said, 'Quit hollering at that dog! That's abuse!' I told her, 'Shut up you big fat ass!' As she continued to scold me for hollering at the dog, the dog got away again and began to chase the neighbor's cat. I had to chase the dog again and when I finally caught him and took him home she was once again there to scold me. So I said, 'Shut up, you fat son of a bitch. I oughta' burn your f'n house down!' The next morning the police came by and handcuffed me and hauled me off to jail. Not because I admitted to anything, but because I had a little bit of pot in my pocket."

Now Al has bought a piece of property out in the country where he can't get into any trouble with his neighbors.

Rod

I was drafted into the United States Army in January of 1968. At the age of 19 I left my hometown in upper Michigan by train for Milwaukee, Wisconsin, where I went through the routine of paperwork, and so on, at the induction center. The next day I left by plane for Fort Campbell, Kentucky, for basic training. I was assigned to Company E, Fourth battalion, First Brigade. At the end of basic training, I received my MOS, 11 Bravo (infantry) and orders for AIT (advanced infantry training)

Rod

at Fort Polk, Louisiana. I left Fort Campbell with some other men from basic training by Greyhound bus for Fort Polk. I remember that on the way there we stopped for a bathroom break in Memphis, Tennessee. There we were shown the balcony of the Lorraine Motel, where Martin Luther King was shot just a few days earlier.

Upon our arrival at Fort Polk we were greeted by a large overhead sign that read "Tigerland." The training center at Fort Polk was geared towards jungle training for Vietnam. I was assigned to Company C, Fourth Battalion, Third Brigade. The scoop was that if you went to Fort Polk you were going to go on to Vietnam as a grunt. At Polk I didn't know anyone. The other guys that were with me on the bus were assigned to other training units. In training I had the highest score in shooting the M-16 rifle in my battalion. I received a

Zippo lighter inscribed with my name and the words, "High score M-16 Cong Killers."

After AIT training I got my orders. I was going to Vietnam. But first a 30-day leave at home. (With 5 days left in my leave, Bobby Kennedy was killed on June 5, 1968.) After my leave I reported to Travis Air Force Base in California. Here I went through more paperwork and shots. Oh boy, the shots! We received multiple shots in both arms at the same time (for yellow fever, black plague, malaria, and others). I also received a shot card which documented that I had received these shots. Then I was given a sheet and pillowcase and I was told to go into the barracks. They predicted that I would be asleep for one day and they were right. I didn't know a soul there; you were on your own going through this process. I left for Nam the next day (June 9) by civilian charter flight, TWA. We stopped in Japan for fuel and then on to Nam. On the approach to Vietnam the voice on the intercom said, "Welcome to Vietnam. On your left is the South China Sea and on your right Cam Ranh Bay." I looked out of the window and there it was, Nam. All the training and all of the crap I had gone through was now here to slap me in the face and say, "Come on GI, you're going to die."

After landing, I stepped out onto the runway in 100 plus degrees heat. The stewardess said, "Be careful, keep your head down, and we'll be back in a year to take you home."

Well, here I was in Vietnam. My feelings at this time were of starting a big adventure. I was standing, staring in the hot sun, like an unblinking baby in its first day out of the womb. I was totally ignorant of Vietnam. I couldn't find it on the map, and I didn't know which way was home—10,500 miles away. A good friend of mine from my hometown was killed in Vietnam just six months before I was drafted. (I think he was in the 173rd Airborne Division). With this knowledge, I knew that it was now my turn to die. Three hundred and sixty five days to go.

In Cam Ranh Bay, the new guys were directed to the replacement center where we filled out more paperwork and were assigned barracks, which were tents with wood floors. In short order, we were divided into small groups to perform work details. The group I was assigned to was told that we would be guards at the base perimeter. We were issued M-14s but without any ammunition. They also gave us old steel pots without helmet liners. Mine had a hole dead front center. Was this an omen?

Cam Ranh Bay was a big sprawling base with all kinds of buildings, clubs, PX, beach, shipping center, and airfield. It was a busy place. The position that we were assigned was a small hole in the sand facing the seaport. At first we were a little scared, but as night wore on it felt as if the army was just messing with us. They were just keeping us busy with mundane, unnecessary tasks. (The NCO in charge said he would bring ammo to us if anything happened.)

All night long, people were walking around us. One guy even had a monkey on his shoulders. They were talking loud, yelling, drinking, and carrying on with women. We learned later that Cam Ranh was one of the safest bases in Nam.

The next day a group of us were shipped by C-30 transport plane to An Khe. Here all replacements began processing and assignment. I found out that I was to be with the First Air Cavalry. (Ever since I had seen that patch on a sergeant in basic, I wanted to be in the Cav so I could wear that patch.) My assignment was First Battalion, Fifth Cavalry (1/5), Air Cavalry, First Cavalry Division, Air Mobile, Alpha Company (A 1/5). At An Khe, there was a mountain and on top of it was painted, in yellow and black, the First Cav patch. It was about 12 inches in diameter. I think the mountain was called Hong Kong Mountain.

During the night there was a mortar and rocket attack on the base. We were told to pull the mattress on top of us if an attack were to occur. In a short while we were rushed to some fortified bunkers. In the distance we could see flashes and hear explosions and being new guys, our imaginations were running wild. In the morning, we were loaded into a Chinook CH-47 helicopter. The ride the day before on the C-130 plane was a first for me and the Chinook was my first helicopter ride. I remember feeling how great it was to fly in one of these. In training back in the states, the only choppers we were in were just mock-ups, a body without blades. The training was to show us how to get in and out of a chopper in seconds. The real getting in and out of a chopper was yet to come (364 days to go…).

From An Khe, we headed to Camp Evans which was a smaller base than An Khe. It was situated in the I Corps (Quang Tri Province). The buildings here were of wood and tents surrounded by sand bags. Gun emplacements were at different locations, 105 mm and 155 mm artillery. These were fortified positions with bunkers surrounding the perimeter. In the middle of the base was a big wooden tower. Here I completed more paperwork and a letter to my parents, along with a form from the division chaplain (that would go to my parents). I was issued a payroll card and I elected to receive only $5 per month for myself. I was advised to do this as where I was going there would be nowhere to spend it. The rest of my pay was to be sent to a bank in my hometown and a $50 savings bond was sent to my parents each month to be used any way they wished. Later on in the afternoon I found out what that big tower in the center of the base was for—me! It was the rappelling and training site, along with a three day combat orientation class site for the First Cav. To me the tower seemed to be 70-80 feet tall.

None of us had ever rappelled before and we had one chance to get it right. We climbed to the top of the tower on cargo ropes. A sergeant on top would hook us up to a D-ring and rope. We would put on gloves, the sergeant would spin us around, tell us to holler "Geronimo," and then yell at us to jump. What a rush! And to think we'll be good enough to do this under fire in combat with just one try. I volunteered to do it a second time. I got the funny feeling since we left Cam Ranh Bay that we meant nothing to anybody or anything. We're worthless FNGs (f'n new guys). During day two at Evans we had incoming mortars and had to jump into fortified bunkers. On the third day I was on a Chinook heading for a place called LZ Jane. (Just 361 days to go.)

Now, this was a ride! I looked out of a small window and down below me was nothing but green jungle. The door gunners on both sides of the chopper were very tense, unlike my ride to An Khe or Evans. LZ Jane was a small firebase in the lowlands close to a big mountain range, the Annamese Cordillera chain. LZ stood for landing zone, and in the cav they were named after the wives of colonels and generals. A good size river ran close to the base. This river provided a water point for the base. Water was purified, hauled into the base and from there it was shipped out to different points in the field. (I got to swim twice in this river later on.)

Low scrub brush and vegetation grew here that got bigger and more dense as you headed to the mountains. Inside of LZ Jane's perimeter were artillery batteries (105 mm, 155 mm and big eight foot guns along with support units). There were many tents, bunkers, and HQ bunkers, communication bunkers, mess tents, and other rear facilities. Everything was surrounded by sand bags. Inside of this the rear echelon people worked, slept and ate. Grunts had a name for them—low quarters or REMFs. The outer edge of LZ Jane had fortified bunkers set apart every 30 meters with small fighting positions between them. In front of the bunkers were strings of razor sharp concentina wire, trip flares, claymore mines, and a few other goodies set out for the enemy in case they came "a callin'." All of the vegetation had been plowed up for a good 50-100 meters for a good field of fire. The LZ (landing zone) was about six to ten acres in size. The landing zone itself was outside the wire and it is here where I first put my boots on the ground. I was told to start walking to where Alpha Company area was. I was about half way there when choppers started landing—many of them. They were called Hueys or Slicks. There were no doors on them and the men sat with their legs hanging out. As they got closer some men on the birds proceeded to stand on the skids. After all of the dust had settled, and the birds flew off, these men started walking in a line by me.

I remember how they looked. They were sweaty, dirty, no spit-shined boots, long hair, unshaven, wearing packs and gear I've never seen before. Their steel pots had camo covers and on these were things such as toothbrushes, bug dope, AK-47 rounds, NVA (North Vietnamese Army) buckles, pins from grenades, short timer calendars, and writing that stated "Make love, not war," "Peace," "FTA," "In God We Trust," and various girls names, aces of spades, peace signs, and many more. The men also had things they had fashioned out of the wood in the jungle—necklaces, bracelets made out of vines, nuts and dried fruit hanging from them and from their rucksacks. Some of their faces were tight and looking straight ahead as they walked by me. A few looked at me standing there in my new jungle fatigues with my duffle bag. One guy in particular looked right at me. I felt that I looked at a man who had "seen the elephant." Eyes unblinking, no expression, but very strong looking—the 1,000 yard stare. I thought, "Man, what kinds of places and things has this man experienced? Gee, I know I'm going to die." I recognized one man who walked by me. He had been in AIT Training with me at Fort Polk. He probably had only been in country for a few more days than I had, and he was already out fighting and looking like a seasoned sky trooper.

At LZ Jane I could hear artillery shells going out from the big guns. Looking out at the mountains I could see jets, planes, choppers, and puffs of smoke coming out of the trees. The war was on and I'm here whether I like it or not. Part of me wants to run and hide, and the other part wants to get it on with the NVA. Let me see what war is really like…after all, you can't kill a Finlander.

The average temperature in the north was 80 degrees and at times, well over 100. The annual rainfall was 79 inches. The humidity was stifling all the time. During the monsoon season it rained day and night for over a month.

The men who had just come into the base were Bravo—First of the Fifth Cav, and were at LZ Jane for a three day stand down. I found Alpha company's rear area and reported in. The first sergeant was gruff and all business. He instructed us to turn in any paperwork that we had and dump our duffle bags. All we would need in the field were the clothes we wore on our back. There were three of us new guys. We hung around the rear area that afternoon. That night we slept on the floor of the first sergeant's tent. We had no blankets, no pillow—just the hard plywood floor. We didn't get much sleep at all. Incoming mortars pounded the area and we had to keep running to the bunkers for cover. The big eight inch guns were firing most of the night. It's impossible to describe how loud these guns were.

When morning came we had chow at the rear mess tent. Scrambled eggs and bacon—the bacon was good, but the eggs were the powdered version. Little did I know that this would be my last hot meal for many months. I also just realized that I hadn't had a shower since I left Michigan.

Alpha Company happened to be at LZ Jane on the last day of a stand down, so after chow I was led to the perimeter to meet my new platoon. I was assigned to the third platoon as an ammo bearer for an M-60 machine gun. I was introduced to the M-60 gunner. He was a black man from Mississippi. He was sitting under a makeshift shelter of ponchos behind one of the fortified bunkers. He ended up being my best friend in Vietnam.

He proceeded to help me gear up. He told me to pack only what I could carry, no extras. I would need a rucksack with aluminum frame, a pistol belt with ammo pouches, a first aid kit with a morphine syringe, an M-16 with two bandoliers of ammo (there were 6 magazines in each bandolier, which would amount to 240 rounds of M-16 ammo). I'd also need a cleaning kit for my M-16, two hand grenades, one smoke grenade, a gas mask, an entrenching tool, a machete with a file, two flares with trip wire, two two-quart canteens and two one-quart canteens, and one bottle of bug dope.

I also had to carry C-rations for five days put into a "chow sock" (a regular GI olive drab sock) which would be tied to the aluminum frame of the rucksack. I also needed to carry a poncho liner, toothbrush, paste, razor, pen and paper, an instamatic camera with two rolls of film, Kool-Aid, a towel, matches, a lighter, three to four packs of cigarettes, a bayonet knife, and a claymore mine. I also found out that the ammo bearer had to carry the extra weight of two M-60 ammo cans. Add to that a loose belt of M-60 ammo (100 rounds) around the shoulder to the waist. All of this gear added up to around 70 pounds or more. That's why they called us "grunts." It came from the sound we made when lifting our heavy pack. The M-60 gunner (which I later became) also had to carry an M-1911 Colt 45 pistol.

I was already sweating profusely and found out that getting enough water was going to be my greatest priority and challenge. After I was all set up the gunner and I sat in a little shelter and looked towards the mountains. I could see and hear the war going on and the gunner said, "Tomorrow we'll be going there." I was introduced to the rest of the platoon and then settled down for a restless night. I kept thinking, "I don't want my arms or legs blown off. I'm not going to make it." My new friend told me to write home now because it would be much harder to do it out in the field. Letters could be mailed to the world free—we wrote free where the stamp would go. He also said that we were not to write a diary or keep in our possession anything that could fall into the enemy's hands and be used against the United States or my family back home. He then said that the NVA (North Vietnamese Army) did not keep grunts as a POW (prisoner of war). The NVA would most likely finish you off, if wounded, by shooting you in the eye at point blank range with an AK-47. Grunts did not have any great value to them.

They also had a history of cutting off fingers first before they blew you away. The best bet if you were badly wounded and in jeopardy of being taken by the NVA would be to save one round or grenade for yourself. I would have done it.

The first time in the field...the way of the cav to go into combat was by chopper. Our company A-1/5, 135 or so strong, were air lifted in choppers called Hueys or Slicks. We were to make a combat assault (CA) into the mountains that my M-60 gunner said would "tear me a new ass." Taking off was great, eight grunts, a pilot, copilot, and two door gunners. Up and away we went. I sat on the floor with my legs hanging out—no doors on these birds! What a feeling—dense jungle below, cool air blowing on my face, the chopper swaying gently with the "whop, whop, whop" sound beating in the background. We were 500-600 feet up on the way out. The ride was short and before long we started dipping down. The ride was now getting more wild. I was hoping that I wouldn't fall out of the chopper. There was nothing to hang onto except the man next to you. Above us were AG-1G Cobra Gunships, called snakes, firing rockets and mini-guns (multi-barreled machine guns capable of firing 2,000 to 3,000 rounds per minute), with every fourth round being a tracer. They were firing into an LZ below us. With this, artillery shells were landing also. This process was called "Prepping the LZ." It was designed to keep the enemy's heads down while we landed in the choppers.

I was in the lead bird and we were to land first. As the last artillery shells hit, we jumped out before the chopper touched ground. Within seconds our bird was off and we were running to the edge of the clearing to pull security for the rest of the men landing behind us. Fortunately, this was a green (or cold) LZ, which meant that no hostile fire or enemy was there to meet us. This was not always the way it went. Within minutes the entire company had arrived and we started to move out by platoons. This is basically the way it went for 12 months. If the LZ was red (or hot) meaning taking fire by landing, it was very scary. My heart would be in my throat, mouth very dry, and spitting cotton. The pit of my stomach would be in a knot.

After heading out, we would "hump" (walking patrols), searching for the enemy. We would patrol and set up day and night ambushes. Just before dark most of the company would set up an FOB. An FOB was a 360 degree perimeter where we dug fox holes and set out trip flares and claymore mines. Every platoon also had to send out LPs (two-man listening posts set out about 50-60 meters from the FOB) and night ambushes. Normally, six to seven men would go out on these. They were scary and deadly.

Alpha Company was humping at the highest part of the mountains. We were in line 20 meters apart between each man when the shooting started. Just two short blasts of automatic M-16 fire. We discovered that our company commander and his RTO were reading maps when two NVA came along the trail in front of them. Luckily the RTO had his M-16 at the ready and got off two bursts. Both NVA dropped dead where they were. Later when we moved up I saw my first dead NVA. They were both lying where they fell. They had already been checked out for paperwork. Their AK-47s had been taken as well as their belt buckles (the belt buckle of the NVA had a red communist star on it and it was a coveted war souvenir for grunts). Watches, rings and anything else the GIs wanted were collected and the bodies were left to the rats and to rot in the hot tropical jungle. As I looked at them I asked one of the men about the bodies. He said a few words about leaving them and then he said, "There it is." ("There it is" and "What it is" are phrases put in front of or behind sentences, and this was the first time I ever heard that.) As I walked away, I thought about how the two dead NVA may have had families, and they would never know their fate. I had to get myself out of this civilian mind set and concentrate on keeping my guard up, scanning left and right, up and down, looking for anything and everything.

Note: From here on my writings will not or cannot be in order of occurrence. Since I did not keep a journal or diary, I can only go on recall that has been clouded after about 38 years and the stress of intense combat. Also, the way I saw and felt things are different from other men because of our personal make up, how long we were in country, how close one was to the action, the angle, state of mind, and so on. I will also refrain from using names for the purpose of their honor and respect for their families. I do have many of men's names, service numbers, hometowns, and dates of death or day wounded for anyone who is searching for information about a loved one. I will use first names for those men pertinent to the story.

We were in a firefight in June 1968 where we killed four NVA and had only one GI wounded. He was a man from Arkansas who was shot in the belly by an AK-47. I will never forget the sound of his scream when he was hit. After we medivaced him out, I walked by where he was shot. There was lots of blood on the ground, cloth cut from his uniform, gauze soaked in blood and the ground was stained purple with "goofy grape" from a smoke grenade. We named the color of smoke grenades after Kool-Aid—Choo Choo Cherry for red, Goofy Grape for purple, and so on. I was thinking, "Man, belly wounds sure must be painful the way he was screaming." It was awful.

Later on in this mission we came upon a place where the ground had been dug up. The smell in the air was pungent with rotting corpses. On top of the ground scattered about were pieces of equipment, clothes and helmets. These were the remnants of a fierce firefight between South Vietnamese (Army of the Republic of South Vietnam—ARVNs) troops, and the NVA. We were told to dig up the recently dug ground and search among the bodies for hidden weapons. This was a very disturbing task. Pieces of flesh and other body parts would come off in our hands. The smell was unbearable with maggots everywhere. We only had entrenching tools and our bare hands to work with, so this mess was inches from our faces. It was determined that they were ARVN troops and the place would be marked on a map for later burial. I was to perform this gruesome task many times during my tour in Vietnam. Following this task, our clothes were stained and covered with the remains that we had just handled. There was no water or no soap with which to clean up with. We moved on, hunting for the enemy.

At a place where we set up one night we were hit with mortars and rockets. Our company commander from Tennessee, Joe, was wounded in the hand. We stayed in our foxholes all night, with no sleep, waiting for a ground attack. One small probe was made by the NVA but that was about it. The next day we found the crash site of a United States Bell chopper (OH-13), also called a "bubble," that had been shot down. The pilot was dead.

A day later, a man from my platoon, a squad leader from California whose name was Bob, was wounded by a booby-trap. He set off a chicom grenade which was hanging on a tree—he tripped the wire and that set off the grenade. Bob was lifted out with an upper leg wound.

In this area where our mission was, I found out that there were many ways to die or to be severely wounded. There were booby-traps of many kinds, trip wires hooked to grenades, C-4 shells from artillery rounds, mortar rounds, bombs of every size (200-500 pounders and bigger), punji pits, and punji stakes dipped in human waste, and many more. You needed a sharp eye and lots of experience to detect these traps of death. You had to be on guard at all times, with little or no sleep. Our "old timers" would constantly tell or show us the ways of the booby-traps. To miss one or step on one could mean death to both you and your fellow grunts. Later that month another man was shot in the belly. I again heard that same terrible scream.

Occasionally a guy would bring out this dog that could sniff out the North Vietnamese (NVA) and knew their scent well. They knew the scent of their urine and their body odor. However, somehow the NVA got hold of some shaving cream and lathered it all over their bodies and hid in holes in the ground. The dog didn't recognize the smell (the dog associated that smell with United States' soldiers) and didn't sniff out the NVA. We walked into a real mess that time. We finally found out that using the dog wasn't going to work for us.

And then we fought in areas where the earth was all burned up from bombs leaving the earth full of craters. The dead forest with the brown leaves all over the ground was probably due to the defoliant (Agent

Orange) which seemed to be sprayed indiscriminately where ever there was heavy canopy forest.

We usually lived on C-rations. They'd been canned during World War II but they were okay. Up until that time we ate K-rations, which were packaged in the 1920s and early 1930s. One day a big meal was sent out to the field to us. It had mashed potatoes and all kinds of things. The potatoes were cold but we didn't care. Later on they brought us ice cream. None of us had eaten ice cream or rich foods for so long that our systems couldn't handle it, and everyone threw up.

Dinner brought out to the field.

From time to time we would have church services out in the field. I always had a lot of respect for the chaplains because their lives were in danger and yet they were there in the midst of it all. One of the chaplains later kept in touch with me. He wrote several books about Vietnam and included stories about my company.

Church services in the field.

When I came home I felt like I had died in Vietnam. I didn't trust anyone and I was always in fights. I was drinking heavily. I had been in a situation in Vietnam where we were airlifted from one hot spot to another. On our way we felt like throwing up from the anxiety.

I wouldn't sit in a place in a restaurant where there were people behind me. I couldn't go anywhere where there were more than two people. I'd blow up over little things. If my wife was driving and she made a wrong turn I'd go ballistic. I slept holding on to the head end bars of the bed all the time because in Vietnam, if I didn't hold on to a tree on a hill during the rainy season, I'd slide through the mud down the hill into the enemy. When I came home I slept with a loaded gun under my bed. Now that I have a grandchild I will get rid of it.

It took me a long time to finally go to counseling. I didn't trust anyone. I would go an hour early and sit outside in the car and cry. I felt like throwing up. I finally got a therapist that I trust completely. He's helped me a lot. I also have a doctor who has gotten me on the right kind of medications. For the first time in years I can sleep at night, and I don't have nightmares. I take sleeping pills at night, but if I take an afternoon nap I will have flashbacks. As soon as I relax and start to fall asleep I get flashbacks.

I used to think about and plan my suicide all the time. I was saving containers of gas in my garage. I planned to fill the swimming pool with sand, pour gas on it, drink some gas, and light a match. I felt like I was dead anyway. I couldn't sleep, and I couldn't lead a normal life. I would go to the movies with my wife and if the seat wasn't in the right place in the theater I'd get up and leave and walk home alone. If I went to church I'd sit and sweat and shake. I didn't want to socialize with other people. My wife had a friend whose husband was in the air force and she wanted to get together and socialize with them. The only people I trusted were army combat veterans so I wouldn't go with her, or try to get to know them. She didn't understand why until recently.

Counseling has opened up the lines of communication between us and now she finally understands why I felt and behaved the way I have in the past. I still have a lot of flashbacks and the things that trigger them are so unpredictable. Recently we had a bad storm. There was lightning, hail, high winds, and the hail and winds were stripping the trees of their leaves. The street was covered with green leaves from the storm. I opened the door and the smell of all the shredded leaves was the first thing I noticed, and "bang," I had a flashback. It smelled exactly the way the forest smelled in Vietnam after a firefight. The bullets would hit the leaves and they were shredded on the ground. I found myself sitting in the rainwater. My son-in-law didn't know what was happening to me.

I had to quit my job because I just couldn't work anymore. I got a job at the post office, delivering by car. I would drive up to a group of mailboxes and put the mail in. One day, as I drove up to deliver some mail, I couldn't get near the boxes because there was a hearse parked in the way. I had to park my vehicle and get out in order to do it. As I was putting the mail in, the coroner and some other people came out of a house with a dead body on a stretcher. They all had gowns, latex gloves, and masks on. A person had died and it wasn't discovered for a week and the body was decomposing. I could immediately recognize the awful smell, and the smell of the body immediately triggered a flashback. In my flashback my body was in many pieces and each piece had eyes and it was in the trees and all over. It was horrible. Eventually I came out of it. I found myself standing next to a large pine tree in the yard and I was sweating and trembling. I was in bad shape. I looked at my watch and 40 minutes had passed since I had gotten to the boxes. I made my way back to my vehicle and called the post office to tell them that I needed some help. They told me there was no one to help me. I was really in bad shape. A retired state police officer came by that I knew and I asked him for some help.

Later that day when I returned to the post office, very visibly shaken, the postmaster came up to me and said, "Through rain or snow, sleet or dead bodies, we deliver the mail." I felt like I wanted to kill him. He was making a joke out of it. I had no idea why I felt or did the things I did. At that time I didn't know that my experiences in Vietnam could alter my life so drastically. No one understood. It wasn't the only bad experience I'd had in the post office. I'd had experiences like this in the past as well as in the future.

Rod was wounded in Vietnam and has many physical problems. He has arthritis and can't turn his head. His hands are stiff. He has hypertension, irritable bowel syndrome, colitis, and realizes now that it is all connected to PTSD. Before he got the courage to come and talk with me he had taken medication to calm down. Up until recently he wouldn't have come at all.

I visited Rod at his home when I interviewed him and was very impressed. He had an exceedingly large amount of history at his home including photographs, memorabilia, and a journal of his experiences. Several books have been written about Vietnam in which Rod has been included. Rod's wife had a special display case for some of the memorabilia and medals, which included two Purple Hearts, a Bronze Star, an Air Medal, and a Silver Cluster that signified five campaigns he had participated in. The Air Medal signified that he had participated in a numerous amount of air assaults. Rod doesn't really care about the medals. He said, "Well, we really weren't medal mongers."

Rod's life has been very difficult for the past 35 years. He became reclusive, thinking frequently about suicide, unable to sleep at night, and haunted by flashbacks and nightmares. He has suffered from a very severe case of PTSD and is still struggling. However, for the first time in years, thanks to counseling and medication, he is able to sleep, enjoys his grandchild, and

THE UNITED STATES OF AMERICA

TO ALL WHO SHALL SEE THESE PRESENTS, GREETING:
THIS IS TO CERTIFY THAT
THE PRESIDENT OF THE UNITED STATES OF AMERICA
AUTHORIZED BY EXECUTIVE ORDER, MAY 11, 1942
HAS AWARDED

THE AIR MEDAL

TO

PRIVATE FIRST CLASS E-3 ROD▒▒▒▒ ▒▒▒▒ ▒▒▒▒▒▒▒ UNITED STATES ARMY

FOR
MERITORIOUS ACHIEVEMENT
WHILE PARTICIPATING IN AERIAL FLIGHT
DURING THE PERIOD JUNE 1968 TO OCTOBER 1968 IN THE REPUBLIC OF VIETNAM
GIVEN UNDER MY HAND IN THE CITY OF WASHINGTON
THIS TWENTY-NINTH DAY OF OCTOBER 19 68

JOHN J. TOLSON
Major General, United States Army
1st Cavalry Division (Airmobile)
Commanding

SECRETARY OF THE ARMY

Rod's citation for the Air Medal.

life is definitely better. "I'd like to get to the point that when I put gas in the lawn mower I think about mowing the lawn rather than pouring it on myself and lighting a match."

Rod told me a story about how on the way home on the plane, one of the guys he'd been with for a year asked if he had any money. The guy was broke. Rod told him that he only had twenty dollars but he could have it, and he gave it to him. Years later at a reunion they got together. The guy hugged him and shook his hand. Rod felt something in his hand, and when he looked, it was a twenty dollar bill.

In the books I read that included Rod he was portrayed as a hero. Rod is remembered by his buddies as an outstanding machine gunner. He is respected by everyone who knows him. He is a very humble man who has definitely paid his dues and sacrificed a lot for his country. Rod is still working to normalize his life. He is making progress and hopefully will find peace and happiness. I am honored to have met him.

Isolated

The following letter gives you an idea of the kind of sadness and turmoil some veterans experience and the helplessness and hopelessness they feel. Names have been changed for privacy reasons.

Dear Sir:

I am writing this because I don't know where to turn. I know I cannot last much longer at the family business. My father passed away on New Year's Eve. Things are falling apart. I cannot cope with the business; the stress and anxiety have me on edge all the time. I can't do this anymore.

Everyone looks to me for answers. I cannot even manage myself; how can I look after others? This point has been coming for a long time. I am sad, guilty, lonely and lost. I have nowhere to turn but to you.

I went to Milwaukee in January for an evaluation. I don't think it went very well. I cried too much and I don't think I told the doctor about work. I am trapped. I can't even type this without crying. What am I supposed to do? I can't work or deal with people.

After I returned from the war I got married and had two babies. I worked as a stock boy and sales clerk for a record store. My wife left me because I was so moody and difficult to live with. I quit the record store. I was depressed and kept to myself most of the time. I remarried and started working for my dad in 1975 at the family business. My brother also worked there. I did maintenance, dishes and helped around the kitchen. I had a hard time dealing with people telling me what to do. I used to yell at my dad or mom, whoever was in charge, and make big scenes.

Over the years, although I was paid a wage, I didn't do much. I think my dad kept me around because he wanted to help me. He was always loaning me money, first for a house and then to keep the business going.

A couple of years ago my brother left the family business. My dad was getting up there in years so then it was up to me to run things. I have stayed out of the daily operations of the business, choosing to spend my time in my office, away from people. The place is pretty much run by the employees. I haven't been a good leader. Last year my second wife left me. She said I abused her emotionally over the years and that she did not love me anymore. I have never intentionally been mean or anything like that. I do not know where the rage comes from. I just want to find a dark hole to hide in. How can I work?

I need to save myself somehow. What will I do? Everything is so hopeless. I can't stop crying.

Signed,

A veteran

Rage

The following was written by a Vietnam veteran when he returned and was beginning his recovery from PTSD. As you've noted from many of the previous stories, everything is a crisis with PTSD, whether it is dealing with traffic, opening the mail, or answering a telephone. Somehow it is all connected with the war and survival.

Today's Rage

Rising like iron ore scaling the callused timbers of the shaft, riding the beltway, the artery of failure and defeat. My blood seethes with streaks of green and black, giving the go ahead. Yet my mind's eye sees the treacherous fall at the apex of the journey and wants no part of it.

Heavy fuel, raging with anger and hate. Out of control for this day's journey, yet it is not a day but a moment.

From the soles of my feet, even through my steel-toed boots, I feel it creep the distance to the ridge of my calf. Uncontrolled yet attached to the flow of the rhythm of my heart. My heart…is it following, or leading the call from below?

Faster now, my legs are on fire, the pit of my stomach aches, bile flows from every port, adrenalin from every other and my heart pounds out the rhythm of the drum, the war drum. My head is silent, the world around me quieted by my acute focus and need to fire the first shot.

The first shot, such an important move. To win I must fire the first shot. Electrifying bolt of fire, excite every cell in my brain, my body. Am I still in control? Is the battle line drawn, am I trapped to follow through with this impending war? Am I right?

Rage. I do not know where it comes from; it scares me sometimes. All the power, the heavy guns with cannon balls and fired tar rest at my lips about to explode.

Then I feel a gentle hand on my shoulder. "You all right, Dad?" he says. I look to him and smile. "Yes, Dan, I am all right." "What you thinking?" he asks. "Oh, I am thinking about getting you to the airport on time. I am going to miss you, you know." "Well, Dad, we have plenty of time, no need to rush. Slow down and get back to the business of driving because as we speak, you are going through a red light." So calmly, so lovingly he speaks to me.

Where was I? Oh yeah, the way some people drive really makes me mad!

Steve W.

Robin

Robin and her husband have both been treated for PTSD as a result of a tour in Vietnam. They previously work with wounded veterans in a veterans' hospital, and Robin recently obtained her master's degree from Northern Michigan University for her work with these wounded, especially those suffering from PTSD. She has generously allowed me to share her story.

Robin was trained as a medic and then a field doc (a clinical specialist) treating the wounded when they returned to the United States from Vietnam. "It was not easy helping these once strapping young men adjust to badly damaged or missing body parts, loss of bodily functions, loss of friends and/or family, and overwhelming grief because they survived."

"Not only did they have physical injuries, they also had mental and emotional ones and feelings of disgrace, guilt, cowardice, and shame." Most of the veterans became dear friends, and one is her husband.

At the time Robin worked in the medical field she had very high ideals. Today she still has nightmares of those days. She still wonders if she did enough or if she did too much. She remembers the young soldier who would not look at her or anyone else. His face was badly scarred and both legs were blown off. He struggled to eat, write, or wash his face with his remaining arm and he could no longer father children. He could not look at his own reflection and wondered why he was still alive. His young son had screamed when he first visited him in his hospital room and he wondered why his wife would want to stay with him. "Too many times I have had to reassure them that at least they were alive. To what purpose? What gave me the right to play God? Sometimes I wonder how I could be so naïve."

Robin's nightmares include witnessing the incompetence both in and out of the military service within the veterans administration, and in public and private hospitals. For example, one surgeon couldn't be bothered with gloves, a gown, or washing his hands after treating an infected patient in isolation before going to tend to a fresh surgical amputee patient. This patient had lost his leg up to his knee but later lost his entire leg, and when she tried to talk to the charge nurse she was told to shut up.

It was agonizing to watch terminal patients suffer because they were not given enough pain medication for fear they would become addicted to it. Nurses and aides were pushed to their physical limits, forced to give patients minimal care, or worse, neglect, because of petty bureaucracy.

Then there is the supposed treatment of the veteran. Certainly support is available, and granted, medically discharged veterans can usually obtain the care they need. However, men and women not medically or psychologically discharged all too often have to fight the bureaucracy to obtain even a modicum of care. This is especially true of Vietnam veterans, both male and female, who have had to struggle to receive treatment for Agent Orange exposure, or appropriate therapy for psychological injuries inflicted not only by the war itself, but by their own countrymen. Family members and former friends telling them to "Get over it," or to "Grow up, already." Family counseling that could possibly save a marriage and a family was put off, as was individual counseling, until the veteran's life was demolished by horrific memories, paranoia, and so forth. This in turn led to substance abuse, physical abuse, incarceration, and/or commitment to an institution, or suicide.

"My nightmares are all too real," Robin says. "My dreams of war wounded made me question whether or not what I had done to save lives had been right. So did witnessing the seemingly never-ending vegetative state of too many patients. I came to question whether or not, they too, should have been allowed to die."

Robin could not handle the lack of compassion or the ineptitude of some of the medical profession. She began to wake up during the night crying and in a sweat. She was showing symptoms of post-traumatic stress disorder. She had nightmares and daymares (nightmarish fantasies while being awake), and at times it became very difficult for her to cope with life from day to day. She would lie in bed trying not to think.

Sometimes she falls asleep but it is not a restful sleep. She finds it hard to get up and get dressed and often doesn't get around to taking her morning medication until noon. She has little appetite or energy. At night she is restless and can't sleep; she tries to read but can't concentrate long enough to read a book. Some nights she'll do puzzles or play solitaire on the computer for hours, afraid to go to sleep, and even more afraid of what she'll wake up to.

Unfortunately, Robin's husband, a Vietnam veteran who put in a tour in Vietnam and also worked in the medical field in the states after serving his tour of duty, also has PTSD. It has been very difficult for Robin to watch his gradual deterioration and decline from the adventurous, fun loving man she married to someone who has difficulty leaving home even to go to church. Only in retrospect does she see the changes and deterioration that took place in him. Firecrackers and fireworks or a car backfiring made him dive for cover. An inability to sleep, along with a breakdown in communication, a deep depression lasting most of a year, were only some of the symptoms she remembers. His energy and ambition had declined, there were cleanliness problems, and a dependency on food to the point of weight gain. He began to isolate himself more and more.

"Almost every time I went home I would find him sitting in a chair under the big pine tree slumped over a bit, sleeping. The lawn was knee high in weeds and some of the grass was waist high. Too often his hair would be greasy and he looked and smelled as if he'd worn the same clothes for days. The proverbial straw was when I came home and found that the dogs had run away and he hadn't bothered to look for them. I found rotted food on dishes and he hadn't taken a bath. He wasn't taking care of himself at all. I told him if he didn't get help, I wasn't coming home again." She got back into the car and left.

That week her husband sought counseling and medical help. In a short period of time he was diagnosed with PTSD and was given a 100% disability. He was given counseling and medication and he has improved greatly, enjoying the chirping of birds, his grandchildren, and the beauty of creation. But he will never stop looking over his shoulder and he will always be on guard. Sharp sudden noises still affect him, making him jump, and at times he is still afraid to open a window curtain for fear someone is drawing a bead on him to shoot him. This is the man who loved to fish and hunt, and served both in his church and his community. He is the man who loved helping his boys with their homework and scouting projects. This is what PTSD has done to one family.

Walking Wounded

The following is taken from Robin's master's thesis. (The same Robin whose story you just read.) It shares, in her own words, why the war in Vietnam was unique and why some of the symptoms of these veterans have been so elusive.

During the Vietnam War, each soldier had his individual beginning and end of combat duty. Each soldier counted how many days longer he had to "hang on." At the top of every letter home, MK, as well as several other veterans I spoke with, wrote how many days he had left. His plans for the future were based on his return to "civilization" and returning to normal life. This attitude deeply affected the soldiers. According to Jim Goodwin, this meant that tours in Vietnam were solitary, individual episodes. "It was rare, after the first few years of the war that whole units were sent to the war zone simultaneously." In other words, even though the soldier was part of a unit, he never felt part of that unit. There was little cohesion with in-country "seniors" leaving with the most experience and "greenies" taking their place. Comradeship was almost nonexistent since what ties were made were quickly broken. Instead of an "army," it was as if each soldier fought on his own.

Nor did the troops return simultaneously. Each soldier essentially came home alone on a plane or jet. He knew few, if any, of the other soldiers flying with him. He felt as if he could not talk about his experiences on that flight or after returning home because no one could possibly understand what he had experienced. Those that could understand were either still in combat or dead. MK said that he didn't know anyone on the flight to Vietnam, nor when he left. When getting ready to leave Vietnam, it was raining so heavily that the departure was repeatedly delayed. In the meantime, the enemy was "walking in a mortar," firing, watching to see where it hit, readjusting the distance, and firing again. He stated, "As the hits got closer, talk about 330 guys suddenly getting religion. The pilot put it in the wind, turning on the afterburners half way down the runway. We had been absolutely silent, but as the plane rose, we all cheered." In spite of this common denominator, the men talked very little en route. And yet, these soldiers were expected to return to "normal life" and somehow forget their experiences.

Why do these warriors continue to have such deep-seated psychological trauma? It seems that the dramatic increase in walking wounded with Vietnam veterans is due to several factors. First of all, one must consider the type of warfare used in Vietnam. This was the first war in which the American soldiers not only seldom knew who or where the enemy was, they were not sure if they knew what they were fighting for; rather than clearly defined battle lines, most of the tactics used by the enemy was guerilla warfare. All too often, any ground gained had to be fought for again, regained, and regained. Traps were set to injure, maim and demoralize. Children were used as weapons by taping or tying explosives to their bodies and sending them to ask for candy from the soldiers; then the explosives were detonated. MK, who was drafted into the Army, stated: "Our base in Pleiku had an underground enemy base (literally under their feet), which allowed (the enemy) practically unlimited access." He also indicated, "The mama san who cleaned your room during the day could be your enemy at night." GL, who enlisted in the army, stated, "You just don't see them. They shoot and then take off. They liked to ambush and retreat cause they knew they were overpowered."

An Expert's Summary of PTSD

Dan Forrester, Ph.D., who has been working for the past 20 years counseling Vietnam veterans, many of whom shared stories in this section, summarizes some of his findings from working with Vietnam veterans suffering from PTSD.

As a seasoned veteran got down to his last two months in Vietnam, he was struck by a strange malady known as the "short-timers syndrome." He would be withdrawn from the field and if logistically possible, would be settled into a comparatively safe setting for the rest of his tour. His buddies would be left behind in the field without his skills, and he would be left with mixed feelings of joy and guilt. Feelings of guilt about leaving one's buddies to whatever unknown fate in Vietnam apparently proved so strong that many veterans were often too frightened to attempt to find out what happened to those left behind.

Some survivors often ask, "How is it that I survived when others more worthy than I did not?" Survival guilt is based in the harshest realities, the actual death of comrades in the struggle of the survivor to live. Often the survivor has had to compromise himself or the life of someone else in order to live. The guilt that such an act invokes or guilt over simply surviving may eventually lead to self-destructive behavior by the survivor. It is not unusual for these men to set themselves up for hopeless physical fights against insurmountable odds. Some may become involved in car accidents. Veterans who often suffer the most painful survivor guilt are those who served as corpsmen or medics. Many of the men they tried to save were beyond all medical help yet they blame their incompetence. It is common for those with survivor's guilt to feel that they do not deserve to enjoy their lives, to find happiness because others didn't make it and it would be dishonoring them by getting on with their lives.

Many Vietnam veterans are very vigilant human beings. Their senses are tuned to anything out of the ordinary. A loud discharge will cause them to start or hit the ground. Many veterans become very uncomfortable when people walk closely behind them. Some are uncomfortable when standing in the open or are uneasy when sitting with others behind them. All these behaviors are survival techniques.

In terms of rage, when combat was experienced in Vietnam, soldiers were often left with wild and violent impulses with no one upon whom to level them. The nature of guerilla warfare with its use of such tactics as booby-traps, land mines, surprise ambushes with the enemies' quick retreat left the soldier feeling like time bombs. The veterans wanted to fight back but the antagonists had long since disappeared. Often they unleashed their rage at indiscriminate targets for want of more suitable targets.

Upon return from Vietnam, the rage that had been tapped in combat was displaced against those in authority. It was directed against those the veterans felt responsible for getting them in the war in the first place and against those who would not support the veterans while they were in Vietnam or when they returned home. The Vietnam veterans left with feelings of guilt for both the outcome of their rage in Vietnam and also those who bore the brunt of the veterans' rage upon their return home, such as family members.

Veterans struggling with PTSD find the hours right before sleep very uncomfortable. Many stay awake as long as possible. They may often have a drink or smoke marijuana to dull uncomfortable thoughts. They have nothing to occupy their minds at the end of the day's activities and their thoughts often wander back to the battle zone. Finally, with sleep, they report having reoccurring dreams about traumatic events. Some do not remember the specific dreams, yet they have a sense of dread about them. They sleep fitfully and often wake up in a sweat. They sometimes call out in agitation. They often wake during the night and end up waking up in the morning still feeling tired. Many of their wives cannot sleep in the same bed with them for fear of physical harm and being subject to disturbing screams and warnings.

Many obsessive thoughts are triggered by everyday experiences that remind the veteran of the war zone. These triggers could include helicopters flying over, the smell of urine, the smell of diesel fuel, popcorn popping, tree lines, the smell of soil, thunder and lightning, a rainy day, and the sight of Asians. Watching the news, TV programs or movies can often trigger memories depending on the content.

Triggers are cues that have become associated with the original trauma. These triggers can be found in twelve different categories:

1. Visual (seeing blood or road kill, black garbage bags)
2. Sound (A backfiring car, thunder, gunshots)
3. Smells (diesel fuel)
4. Taste
5. Physical or Body
6. Significant dates or seasons (anniversary dates of trauma, holidays, rainy season, dates when going and returning from war zone)
7. Strong emotions
8. Thoughts
9. Behaviors
10. Out of the blue (sometimes intrusions occur when you are tired or defenses are down.)

11. Stressful events

12. Combinations (often triggers contain several memory aspects at once)

It is important to recognize the importance that triggers have in the activation of PTSD symptoms. Treatment focuses on identifying triggers and education about the process which is stimulated by a trigger. Also how to both prevent this process from occurring as much as possible but also what do to when intrusive memories have been activated.

Iraq

Post-traumatic stress disorder did not stop with the war in Vietnam. Even the world's most advanced technology cannot change the scars and memories of war, as we can see from the stories of soldiers returning from Iraq.

Chris

I started in the National Guard, the 107th Engineer Battalion, when I was 18 years old. When I got out I went to college. I got married and then graduated from Northern Michigan University in December of 2004. It was a good year. I was married for a year when I received a letter calling me out of inactive duty. I got orders to report to Fort Benning, Georgia, for training for Operation Iraqi Freedom. I was 29 years old and had planned to work on my master's degree, but I was to report to Fort Benning or go to jail.

Chris

I was tossed in the Army Reserve (Interactive Ready Reserve). I left on April 1 for theater-specific training. I had two weeks of training at Fort Benning. Guys were going to either Africa, Cuba, Afghanistan, or Iraq. We flew from Columbus, Georgia, to Shannon Ireland, to Italy, to Kuwait.

As a deployed individual I was mixed up with a lot of people. At one point there were 1,000 people staying in a huge warehouse type building. Our bunks were a foot apart and there were different units: army, marines, and others.

My MOS was combat engineer, basically infantry. We did demolitions, booby-trap disarmaments, moved obstacles, and put up road barriers. It was what I had learned in boot camp at Fort Leonardwood.

We would wake up at 5 A.M. and go out to a massive, disorganized formation. They would yell out 20 names and say, "You guys are leaving at such and such a time." If your name wasn't called you sat around and dealt with the 120-degree heat and waited.

Finally they told me I was going to Mosul, the third largest city in Iraq. It was just on the border of the Kurdish control area and it was a hot spot at that time. We left on a C-130 cargo plane, flew north over Iraq, and arrived at 2 A.M. The airport was constantly under mortar fire so our plane ride was quite erratic. We had to circle, dive down, come up—it was like a roller coaster ride so the terrorists couldn't mortar our plane. When we landed we had one duffle bag in front and one in back. We then had a healthy jog with everything we were going to live with for the next year.

We sat in a holding place, with a cot, for one and a half days wondering what we were going to do. There were lots of mortar rounds going off but they seldom hit anything. I was with a reserve component from Indiana, about 500-600 people. Things would have been better if I had been healthy, but I wasn't. I have Marfan Syndrome, which is a connective tissue disease.

In my job we had three basic missions. The first mission was Buffalo IEV (improvised explosive devices) Missions. We were trained on a massive, tall, geometric shaped truck with eight inch thick glass and angles that deflect explosives. It had an arm that had devices that could grab and cut.

The second mission was to build a 10 foot tall burm of dirt around the whole city, which was 78 miles long. Mosul is near Syria and insurgents were coming in through the desert and driving into the city. Our infantry patrolled it. Mosul is the city that Saddam Hussein's children were caught in.

The third mission was to protect the local and national elections in 2005. We would go out in night missions from 10 P.M. to 5 A.M. There was a curfew in the city from 9 P.M. to 5 A.M. until the morning prayer. At 5 A.M. all the mosques would play a morning prayer song. You could hear it 10 miles outside of the city.

I ended up being a 50-caliber gunner on a gun truck. During the election we went out and a couple of semi trucks were used as protection barriers at mosques, elementary schools, and polling sites. We had to put up five foot barriers and design entrances to avoid improvised explosion devices (IEDs). The elections turned out well and there were only two interruptions.

There were only two incidents of firefights I was involved in. It seemed like a long time but was actually only ten minutes. I witnessed three deaths—two civilians, and a combatant. I don't know where the combatant was from, possibly Syria or Iran. I was awarded a Combat Action Badge for those incidents; a long knife with leaves around it signifying that it was for combat.

We had to go door to door looking for weapons. You didn't know who was the enemy; it could be the person whose hand you were shaking. You never knew who you could trust. It was an urban environment with narrow streets and gutted out buildings. We were shot at a lot and didn't know where anything came from. Hypervigilance? You had to be on such high alert for 10-12 hours a day. Outside of the wire of safety you're so intently looking and listening for things that could kill you.

Half of the trucks were armored and protected and half weren't. We would try to improve the vehicles that weren't armored by welding any metal we could on them. We called it hillbilly armor. I wondered why some people were so protected and others weren't. Fifty of us wrote home to our families about our unprotected trucks and there were news stories in the Indiana papers. A few weeks later our vehicles were fixed.

One incident that was unpleasant was when we had a pet (stray) dog we all liked and were feeding. It brought a little joy to us. One day an officer shot the dog...no explanation. He just came and shot the dog. I have two dogs of my own and they are like my kids.

It was 120 degrees and we had to dress in flak jackets, basically a vest with heavy metal in it, that weighed 40 pounds. We had long sleeves and had to carry ammo gear, smoke grenades, and two canteens of water.

There was a garbage dump the size of a football field near us. I was on a list for depleting uranium. Even as a gunner I was constantly inhaling dust, and there was raw sewage running on the streets. You'd get shit water sprayed on your face.

I came home on January 6, 2006. We were flown to Kuwait where they had "decompression time" for seven or eight days. We were ordered to play baseball, softball, football and "have fun" in 100-degree weather. It was supposed to be recreation time so you could go back to your family in a good mental state. I didn't enjoy it at all.

We flew into Indiana and there was a three day out-processing where we were all asked a lot of questions and had to turn in our gear. There were thousands of people there being processed in and out. I then flew home to Marquette, Michigan. I was officially discharged and I was happy to be home.

For two to three weeks life was normal and lots of fun. I visited with my mom and dad, played with my dogs, and everything seemed unbelievable. After a few weeks I didn't feel comfortable anymore. It was not normal. I physically, socially, and mentally wanted to isolate myself. Then I turned to binge drinking for a month and a half. I put myself into detox and stopped drinking.

I have nightmares constantly. I take sleeping medication (trazedone). I have flashbacks that are more like daydreams. I have severe mood swings and can go from everything's okay to the whole world collapsing in a minute. I have an obsession with what's going on in Iraq and I'm on the Internet and watching the news constantly. I've been told by my doctor not to watch the news, but it's almost kind of self-abusing behavior that brings about an adrenalin rush. I know it's not a good thing. I have been diagnosed with severe depression and anxiety disorder with anxiety panic attacks. My doctor feels that I'm still living (stuck) in Iraq. I have no interest in anything. I am always tense, always hypervigilant. I feel a lot of anger; driving, the news, everything pisses me off. I am in a constant state of agitation. I feel stone cold as far as my emotions. I can't laugh and I can't cry.

My medical doctors are angry that I was sent to Iraq in the first place because of medical problems I had before I left the country. I can't believe they even accepted me. I talk with a psychiatrist on TV via teleconference at the VA Clinic. All of my problems have affected my marriage. There is a problem with communication and the relationship with my wife has been affected emotionally and physically. I am trying to get better and trying to function, but it's hard. Before I went to Iraq I attended college full time and worked. I tried to go back to work and couldn't handle the people, the noise, or the problems. I take long drives to nowhere just to isolate myself, and when I am at home I isolate. I don't feel comfortable. I was much more social before I went to Iraq.

Recently I had two spells, one at a large store where I fainted and had to be taken to the hospital by ambulance. The other time I was at Presque Isle Park and I went into a panic attack-flashback while in my car. I don't know how I got to the emergency room at the hospital. The Jaws of Life had to open my car door.

My blood pressure had plummeted. They don't know exactly what caused the attack.

I often think about how life would be if I could have just continued on at school and gotten a masters degree. I would have been completed with it by now. My plans have been put on hold. I've tried going back to school but I can't handle it.

You don't need a leg missing or wounds to be injured. I've had to travel away from here to a VA hospital 12 times for medical care and it costs me $120 each time. The VA reimburses me 14 cents a mile. I've been given a 60% disability (10% for medical and 50% for PTSD). I am only 30 years old and have to live on social security because I am unable to work. I need to use oxygen at times and my health has gotten worse.

Chris sees a counselor on a regular basis and the counselor he sees has been very helpful to him and an advocate for him. He calls Chris at home to see how he is between appointments.

The first time I met Chris, a tall handsome young man with brown eyes, his hands were shaking and it was apparent that it took everything for him just to get here and talk with me. Though visibly affected by the war, he is a very likeable person.

I thanked Chris for coming to my home to talk with me. My husband told him if he ever needed someone to talk to or transportation to call or stop by anytime. As I watched him get into his car with his two dogs, Clyde and Rudy, who sat patiently waiting for him, I felt sad. I hope and pray that he will recover and find peace and happiness in the near future.

Like Chris, there are thousands of veterans coming home, many of which are going to need some type of help. The system is filled up. These guys have paid their dues and the funding may not be there to help them.

A dog and a flag, waiting to welcome a veteran home.

On January 6, 2008, Chris passed away. He died unexpectedly of an aneurism. He leaves behind his wife, Kimberly, his parents, his sisters, and other family members.

Chris loved to hunt and fish and ski. He was a talented artist and he enjoyed walking his two dogs, Clyde and Rudy.

May he rest in peace.

Kim

My husband is an Iraq veteran. We had been married for a year before he was called up. It was a good time in our lives.

I always knew what PTSD was because I'd seen it in the news, so I was aware of it, and we figured it out quickly. It first became apparent in our phone calls. He was quick to anger and focus on negative things. When he came home he was sick with flu-like symptoms for three months. It took a few months of adjusting and it later became more obvious. There was a quickness to anger and an irrational response.

He is illogical at times and there is a huge increase in social anxiety. He isolates. He has an exaggerated startle response, where if you drop something…well, it's almost like a frightened animal cowering. I feel he is going down hill. We deal with it from day to day.

Kim's husband passed away on January 6, 2008, at the age of 31.

Noah

What could be more heartbreaking than the loss of your child? We worry about our children as they grow up. We protect them, we hurt when they hurt, and we are delighted in their successes and happy moments.

Noah

When a young adult is sent off to war it adds gray hair and takes years off of a parent's life. We worry and wait for the days to pass until they are safe at home again. Imagine sending your child off to war not once, but twice, for a second or a third tour of duty. Cheryl saw her 18-year-old son go off to Iraq twice. Her son Noah finally returned to safety and she was able to breathe a sigh of relief at last.

Noah said that he thought he had the perfect childhood and that his mom was awesome. He loved to hunt with his dad and fish with his friends, to pick on his sister. He was easy going and loved to joke around. He was kind and sensitive and after the 9/11 attack in New York he decided that he wanted to serve his country. He was a young man at the beginning of his life ready to do the right thing.

He had a lot of courage and served two tours of duty in Iraq. During this time he experienced the horrors of war, witnessing death and seeing innocent people killed. He loved the children and it bothered him to see them in danger or hurt. He survived the bombs and snipers, but the children and the horrors of that war haunted him and filled him with guilt.

He had been trained for war and always followed orders, but after the second tour of duty things had happened that disturbed him terribly and he was changed for life. Physically he had come home in one piece, but emotionally and psychologically he was scarred, and his heart was broken. He became depressed and began to self-medicate with the help of alcohol. Noah had always loved life, but he came home changed. His parents, his friends, and all who knew him could sense that there was something eating away at him. He was not the same person—something was on his mind.

Noah was diagnosed with PTSD. He went in for counseling appointments a few times, but then began to miss appointments. His family worried and tried to encourage him to continue with the counseling and get help. As many veterans with PTSD do, Noah saw counseling as a sign of weakness and thought he could deal with all of this himself. He had no idea how serious PTSD is. He was having nightmares and suffered from guilt. He didn't know that there was a link between these symptoms and the devastating effects he witnessed and experienced in Iraq. But he would try to reassure his mother and said "Ma, you worry too much. I'm fine, I'm happy." However, he had experienced too many horrors of war, and the pain and invisible wounds inside were too much for him to endure. On July 26, 2007, Noah found a secluded spot in the woods and took his own life. The same spot he used to hang out with his friends while growing up and doing the normal boy stuff, like skipping school and going fishing. He took his life in a place that was filled with good memories for him.

Noah's parents are heartbroken. A kind of sadness has engulfed them. Noah is in the loving arms of Jesus now and he suffers no more. He is finally at rest. But they miss him. They ask themselves, How could this have happened? Noah loved life. Only those who have been to war can know the secret knowledge that no ordinary citizen can imagine or understand. The trauma they are left with cuts deep into the soul. The veteran, rather than thinking about it, or dealing with those memories, tries to bury them and forget. But there are triggers that are constant reminders of the pain they endure. A smell, a sound, or the Fourth of July fireworks will bring them back to that experience in a second. The veteran has a difficult time readjusting to civilian life, knowing what is going on in Iraq, and he cannot forgive himself.

It is said that approximately 21 percent of Iraq veterans, approximately 18 veterans a day, four times the national average, commit suicide. Cheryl, Noah's mother, is working on a bill that would make it mandatory that all combat infantrymen be assessed for and treated for PTSD. It would be something the soldier would have to sign and agree to before going into the armed forces. She feels that Noah was a man of his word and would have definitely agreed to counseling if he had signed something prior to entering the service. He deserved help. It was not his fault. He had served his country and he paid the ultimate price. The added bill to the military contracts would be called "Noah's Clause" if Cheryl has her way. Noah died so people would learn about PTSD and Cheryl, his mother, wants to make sure that another family does not suffer like hers has…to make sure another sister is not left without her brother, a father without his son, and a mother never to hold her child again in her lifetime.

The local Amvets Post 33 in Virginia, Minnesota, has been named in honor of Noah. Hopefully, thanks to Noah and his family, the future veterans who come here will be made aware of PTSD and how serious this disorder is and will deal with the symptoms and get counseling. A few already have expressed their thanks to Noah.

Noah's family loved him very much and they know that he did not die in vain regardless of how he died. He died to get the word out to others about PTSD. His name will live on long after we are gone. His family says, "He will always be our hero, just like he was the day he was born."

The following two poems were written by Noah.

Friends

I feel bad for the kids
Can't blame them for begging
Can't give them anything, they beg more
This one was different
He was 7
I let him sit next to me on the Bradley
I give him water,
He goes gets me food.
It's great compared to MREs
No english
No arabic
Yet we still understand each other
Then it's time to leave
He wraps his arms around me crying
I say it will be ok
I still wonder if he is.

Still at war

Got home almost a year and a half ago
We were so happy
That beer never tasted so good
Iraq was the farthest thing from my mind
That was the best week of my life
It crept up slowly
first just while sleeping
more real and scary than when it happened
After, it's on the mind awake
Never 10 minutes goes by without being reminded
Been home a year and a half physically
Mentally I will never be home.

Iraq Veteran

I have a hard time going to sleep. I have been restless. The worst dreams are things that happened over there. I had an amazing reception when I returned home.

I have terrible anxiety. If I hear anything while I am studying, I could just explode. I haven't talked to anyone. No one would understand. How could they? I feel like I've been drinking too much. I feel distant from my feelings and experiences here. I'm always on edge especially when I'm driving. I'm looking for bad things to happen. Bad things happened when we drove in Iraq. There is not a lot of satisfaction in my life right now. I avoid crowds. I don't trust people. I have difficulty expressing feelings.

I hate my job and all the people I work with. They jerk me around and sometimes I'd like to blow someone's head off. It's hard to concentrate and they keep piling on the work. It's a dog-eat-dog world and I don't trust my boss. I know he's made me look bad and doesn't give me credit for anything. I only got credit for things that went wrong. I can't work for someone I don't respect.

Where's the Real You?

I was listening to National Public Radio one day when they interviewed a young woman who had met her husband at a friend's wedding. He was a sweet, sensitive guy who loved to party. Soon after they met, and just before he was sent to Iraq, they got married.

When he finished his tour in Iraq he was asked to fill out a form with questions about his health, particularly things such as nightmares, sleep problems, depression, and so on. Like most of the veterans, he was so anxious to go home he didn't bother to accurately answer the questions.

When he arrived home he was very distant and emotional, not the same person his wife remembered. He kept the blinds closed all the time and didn't want to do anything. He wasn't able to make phone calls, write checks or do other routine things. He became withdrawn. His marriage was in serious trouble and he became suicidal. He skipped appointments at the VA clinic and drove his motorcycle 100 mph, driving recklessly. He was afraid if he went for help a diagnosis of PTSD would make him look weak, like a failure.

Eventually he was persuaded to seek treatment and completed a 24-week program, but he is not the same person. Occasionally the real person seems to come through, said his wife, but for the most part he is dealing with a lot of emotional and psychological problems that may never completely go away.

Comparing Iraq and Vietnam

In comparing the experiences of veterans in Vietnam and Iraq, Dr. Dan Forrester shares the following insights.

Several similarities exist in the general dynamics of both the Vietnam War and the Iraq war. To begin with, they both began with what was thought to be a clear objective but over time became more difficult to define, with a clear objective more elusive. In the Vietnam War, it supposedly began with an attack on an American ship in the Gulf of Tonken. In Iraq, it supposedly began with "weapons of destruction." In Vietnam, the objective became to stop the domino affect of communism. In Iraq, the object has become to bring democracy to the Iraqi people and to fight terrorism. As the war wore on in Vietnam, the objective seemed to be less important than simply surviving one's tour of duty and returning home. At the same time, the patience of the American people seemed to be exhausted, with resentment for the war now being turned towards the soldiers themselves. As Dean Rusk, the Secretary of State, stated later after the war was over, "We estimated the resolve and the ability of the enemy and over-estimated the patience of the American people."

The Iraq War has shown signs of affecting the patience and the resolve of the American people. There has been a growing sentiment to remove American troops from Iraq.

The impression of the American people to the Vietnam veteran was that they lost the war in Vietnam. Similarly, the growing sentiment about the Iraq war is that the American troops will be withdrawn without effectively accomplishing the perceived goals. It is a tribute to the Vietnam veteran that because they endured the resentment of the American people, some of the American people are not making the same mistake by putting their frustrations onto the Iraq veterans. This has been a lesson learned by the American people and generates quite probably from a desire to make up for the mistake of the past, and so the Iraq veteran has had a welcome homecoming with open public support and gratitude. Actually, as a bi-product of this support, Vietnam veterans who wear recognizable veteran's hats, jackets, or have veteran's license plates on their cars are also receiving words of gratitude. This generates mixed feelings by Vietnam veterans who have waited many years to be recognized and appreciated. For some it is "too little, too late." So the anger continues.

One area that looks like it has improved since Vietnam is the period of normalization, the time when veterans are given a "buffer" between their service time and their time returning home. According to a Vietnam veteran, "I requested that I be allowed to spend some time state side at Fort Campbell Army Base for a period of normalization after a year in Vietnam. I knew something was wrong with me and I wasn't ready to go home yet. I'd just left Vietnam." The veteran was given a choice of going home or to re up for another year. Normalization was not an option. "So I lived a kind of dysfunctional life for 35 years," he said, "which very much affected my wife and children. I am healing now and attend counseling sessions every week, but I can't undo the past and all of the damage I've done."

At the present time Iraq war veterans are being brought to a United States base for a period of time, a time to normalize and receive treatment if needed, which might prevent a lot of the problems other veterans have dealt with. Hopefully, families of Iraq war veterans will not have to suffer the frustration and anxiety of living in a dysfunctional family.

Korea

JIM

Jim is a very distinguished and intelligent man. He was born in 1932, graduated from high school in 1951, and in December 1952 he was drafted. He did his basic training in Camp Atterbury, Indiana, from January to March that year, which prepared him for the cold, harsh environment he would endure in Korea. He had a two-week bivouac living outside and sleeping in a pup tent at night. The discipline he learned in the service has helped him throughout his life. Here's how Jim relates his story.

Jim

I was on a train for Fort Lewis, Washington. Two weeks later I was in the Far East. I traveled in a troop ship, where the bunks were stacked six high. During our travel we endured a terrible storm. A lot of the guys got sick and all I could smell was vomit and fuel oil. Things got continually worse. In Pusan, Korea, we traveled by train. The train had uncomfortable wooden seats, no glass in the windows, and the coal smoke blew into the train car from the engine.

Memories of the children still occupy my mind every time I go to a restaurant and see the heaps of wasted food. To this day I can't stand to see food wasted as it reminds me of the starving Korean children with their big brown eyes waiting at the exit of the mess tent for scraps of leftover food. Some of the children rigged up cans on a long stick and would scoop up a can full of slop from the slop cans. It was probably a mixture of cold cereal, eggs, pieces of bread soaked in coffee, juice and milk. The cans had holes in the bottom so the excess liquid could drain out. What was left was the food they ate. When I see food wasted today I see the hunger in those children's eyes.

I was in a place called the punch bowl of Korea, which was located in northeast Korea. I was in the 45th Infantry Division, the 180th Infantry Regiment, Company H. There were bunkers (bag and log bunkers) which were probably cooler in the summer and warmer in the winter, but they were infested by rats, mice, and bugs. I didn't have a bunker to sleep in, and so I slept in a pit that was dug to fill sandbags.

The first night I was in a combat situation the outpost was totally surrounded by Chinese, who were mortaring us. I was assigned to a piece of land and was told, "If you can't shoot 'em, stick 'em." I found a big hole in the ground and stood in it. All hell broke loose. I was working with a squad of guys. A guy who was wounded fell down in the hole and hit me as he fell. I was initially frightened, but when the guy went down I got angry. From then on you change from what you were to what you want to be. I was angry, and I'm still angry. I just wanted to kill Chinamen.

That first night I sat on my helmet in a trench and fell asleep. I awoke to a buzzing sound. Flies were eating the blood of the guys that were killed the night before. It was a mixture of blood and mud, and a helmet with a bullet hole lay on the ground. There was a trench line to his left, which had a putrid smell of decomposing flesh and blood. I was confined in this trench with Chinamen all around me. And you gotta shoot 'em. It's amazing what you can do when you gotta do it. I felt bad. I got all these medals, but I felt bad…What happened to the fifth commandment? I've asked God for forgiveness.

I worked with that squad for a week or two. Then they needed someone to work on 1812 heavy weapons, a weapon that's a direct fire and is two and a half feet long. I threw a round in the chamber and I tapped the gunner on the helmet to signal him that it was okay to shoot. I happened to look up as he shot that round off and just then I looked up and noticed that there was a female Chinese nurse looking right at me. She turned around and went into the bunker, and the round followed her and went right in after her. I said, "Lord, Almighty!" I don't remember any explosion or anything anymore. I still feel a lot of sadness about it. I don't know why they had these female nurses out there. I was raised to put females on a higher level, but she was not on a higher level because she checked out with a lot of others. You'd see short rounds coming in and people killed and injured. The meaning of life seemed like, "What the hell, so what?" The whole value system changes and the benchmarks were all changed.

Jim in Korea, standing third from left in back row.

So this is the way it is and I don't see any value in it. It's so tragic that people have to live that way.

I think the military knew exactly what they were doing and they knew that many of us would react exactly the way I did. I got angry and did exactly what I was trained to do. If people knew what they were going to get into I think they would head the other way.

I remember going into the battalion aide station, which was just a hole in the ground with a lantern up on the ceiling and two 50-gallon drums where we would place the stretchers, and I'd look into the faces of these medics. It was hopeless, just hopeless. You bring these guys in and they're shot up and these guys aren't magicians, ya' know. The medic's faces showed sheer fright and helplessness as they were brought wounded soldiers, brought in with a bullet hole in the head that were far beyond help.

I didn't want to talk about it. If someone were to ask me a question I don't know how I would even describe this. It took me many years to even talk about it. I don't think people would be prepared to hear about it. It's like if you can't say anything good, don't say anything at all. I guess I stuffed it and considered it a bad dream. And I went on.

After Korea I went to school at Michigan State University and got married and worked for the Department of Natural Resources. Subconsciously I was dealing with a lot. I'm still very angry. If someone pushes me too far I get angry, but I will leave. I try to avoid confrontations. Your body changes (after experiencing trauma) and I feel anger now rather than fear. I don't like crowds but I can tolerate them. Certain smells trigger your subconscious, like coal trains and certain sounds such as "clicks." The click of a bolt in a rifle will hyper alert me. Things I don't expect, like a bird flying by or a butterfly, alerts me. It's a trigger. My subconscious is still protecting me. It says, "It happened to you before so why couldn't it happen again?" Its hypervigilance and you're on guard. But you've got to learn to live with it. So I went to school. I was kept busy. I didn't think there was anything wrong with me. I might have been a little tougher and I always did what I was told. I went to work and it was challenging and I enjoyed my work. I didn't sleep too well and I worked too much. I became a workaholic. I had gone from one uniform to another, from an army to DNR uniform. I guess I ran my job like a military unit.

Everything went well until I retired. All of my coping mechanisms failed, and I started stealing things from large stores. I would steal little things like a box of screws or toothpicks. I got pinched a few times and my wife was with me one time. She was real alarmed.

She got me to see a psychologist because she figured something was really wrong. The psychologist diagnosed me with PTSD. She was a real good psychologist and treated me for a year. I saw another VA psychiatrist for a couple of years. They were all good. They helped me to understand what was going on. I don't always remember stealing things and I didn't know why I was doing it. It was hard on my wife and so she had to go for help, too. It was humiliating and I had to go before a judge. I had to learn to develop better coping skills. I got a misdemeanor. I went through four years of psychiatrists and psychologists. The medication they prescribed was good. I could sleep and not have terrible dreams. I'd had very little rest and the drug trazedone helps you to sleep.

What was causing me to steal things? The doctors told me there were several reasons. My body yearned for adrenaline and stealing gave me that adrenaline. I viewed big stores as the enemy and I was still fighting the war. I usually did it on anniversary dates—dates that were particularly traumatic while in Korea. I was also trying to punish myself—a kind of penal system.

So once you know what's going on you don't go to stores or put yourself in risky situations. Contradictions—knowing right from wrong—the mind has trouble with that. I've always attended church and know the commandments and have tried to lead an honest life, and yet I've discovered that the things I had to do in Korea were basically against my character and beliefs.

When I would go to the psychiatrist he talked about feelings. I can't equate to any of that. What's a feeling? I'm numb. Not too much affects me. I get angry fast, like when I'm driving. I can feel emotions with children but other than that…I'm trying to develop sensitivities. I am trying to get patient. I am doing better.

I go to support group meetings from time to time for "tune-ups," as I call them.

Jim has a wonderful wife and five children. I felt much honored to have met him and that he allowed me to interview him.

A very real account of the experiences of Jim and his fellow Korean veterans, along with a history of the Korean War (often called the "Forgotten War"), can be read in the book, *Christmas In July*, written by a group of veterans. It was coauthored by Donald (Hank) Niol and includes personal experiences of Christmas Hill in 1953. It is definitely a book worth reading and will awaken in its readers the reality of war.

Jimmy Boy

I hit the line in 1953, at twenty years of age.
My orders were "to hold my ground, if I couldn't shoot 'em—
     stick 'em!"
I shut my mouth and "wet" my pants.

The bloody trench and sandbag bunker became my home!
I shut my mouth and started shooting!

The flares are up, night is here, "On your feet and off your rear,
The chinks will soon be here!"
I shut my mouth and keep on shooting!

Night after night the Chinese come, they hit us hard, we shot
     them down!
I shut my mouth and keep on shooting!

Night after night my buddies fall beside me, I can't stop this
     insanity!
I shut my mouth and keep shooting!

The smell of blood is in the air, the stench of death is every-
     where!
I shut my mouth and keep shooting!

Hurry to the medics the injured go, their helpless faces I see,
I can't stop this misery!
I shut my mouth and keep on shooting!

Night after night as the fighting ends, to the aid station the
     injured go,
I see medics with "crazed faces glow," no time to falter—no
     way to stop this endless slaughter!
I shut my mouth and keep on shooting!

Mornings after on my helmet I sit, looking at the pools of
blood...I tire,
The buzzing flies, and the commo wire!
I shut my mouth and keep on shooting!

Day after day new boys come. "Jim," I'm told, "Keep an eye on
them."
They too fall one by one!
I shut my mouth and keep on shooting!

I fear no more, no place to flee, for anger, hatred and revenge
Abide in me!
I shut my mouth and keep on shooting!

The trench is drenched with American Boys' Blood,
A sacred place it is to me!
I shut my mouth and keep on shooting!

I fear no more if death should come, this living "hell" is far
from won.
I shut my mouth and keep on shooting!

Ordered off the line July 26, 1953, "No," said I, "Many more
Chinese must die"—
We lost our battlefield efficiency!
I shut my mouth and left the line!

A civilian I became, a workaholic too, could exhaustion ease the
pain?
I lived for the present, suppressed the bad memory—
A loving wife now, with a family!

Forty years of work have passed and a retiree I became,
In trouble with the law of theft, was added to my fame!
I ponder now to sift things out, to assess, to evaluate!

Psychologists say, "Jim, chronic PTSD you surely have!"
I listen now to understand, what's PTSD anyhow?

The fear, anger, and hatred of 40 years ago, are still with me,
Wherever I go!
I listen and shoot no more.

Is PTSD a punishment for causing death and pain?
If so, is surviving really worth the gain?
I listen now and shoot no more!

I live in daily shame, since a cold-blooded killer I became!
I listen now, I shoot no more!

Why do I feel such guilt for I survived, when others were
    killed?
I listen now and shoot no more!

What once was wrong, somehow is right, how can this be?
Please, explain to me!
I listen now I shoot no more!

If what my country said was good, blest by the church as well,
Why do I feel so bad, for being in that trench of hell?
I listen now and shoot no more!

To psychologists, my wife and I do drive,
For I must learn how to "feel" now, at age 65!
I listen now I shoot no more!

From books I'm learning better "coping" skills, to improve my
    character!
I listen now I shoot no more!

New improved attitudes I must learn, "Be Positive, not
    Negative!"
I listen now I shoot no more!

I try to understand "emotions" of love, happiness and to be
  glad,
I know too well those of anger, fear, and to be sad!
I listen now I shoot no more!

This numbness now I try to free, it seems to want to hang on to
  me.
I listen now, I shoot no more!

To PTSD sessions I weekly go, I help some, and others help me.
I learn understanding, compassion, and reality!
I listen now I shoot no more!

I hear words that say, "accountable" for my actions, "needs" to
  be met,
We all make "choices," and that we're "OK!"
I listen now I shoot no more!

From time to time I wallow in despair, perhaps in time
A miserable bastard I'll cease to be! I think this process is called
Therapy. I'm not so sure; I hope it leads to Recovery!
I listen now and I shoot no more!

We hear today some words that say, "Freedom isn't Free,"
And "All wounds don't bleed." Remember when you hear
  these words,
They surely all are true, I verify, I testify, and pass them on to
  you!
And in conclusion let me say, one thing's for sure, and that I
  know,
I listen now and I shoot no more!

LOOK MOTHER, what your "JIMMY BOY" turned out to be—
TO KEEP OUR COUNTRY FREE!

Sergeant James M. Hein, United States Army
45th Infantry Division, 180th Infantry Regiment
Christmas Hill, Korea, 1953

World War II

George

The United States Flag that had draped the coffin was folded and presented to the family. At age 85, cancer of the lung and bones had finally won the last battle.

As the church was filled with voices singing "How Great Thou Art" the coffin was slowly leaving the room. The family was leaving and would accompany George to the cemetery. All of a sudden there was silence in the church. No one uttered a word as the guns of the honor guard fired a salute and a bugle played taps.

The funeral, as funerals go, was beautiful. George had planned it well. Psalm 23 was read, we all celebrated communion, and a Finnish mandolin player sang "Amazing Grace" in the Finnish language. Later we all sang it in English. His grandchildren tearfully gave a beautiful eulogy for the grandfather they dearly loved. He had been the best grandfather you could ever hope for. All of George's favorite songs were sung, including "Children of the Heavenly Father" and "How Great Thou Art." Right down to the lunch menu George had planned his funeral. He was proud of his Finnish heritage, and loved his God and his church. Although he seldom, if ever, spoke about his experience in the United States Army, he was proud to have served his country.

Weeks before his death I had visited George at the veterans hospital in Marquette, Michigan. We talked about many things and I had enjoyed my visit with him and his wife and children. George's first wife had died years ago and he had met a sweet woman who loved him and shared his last ten years with him. As I held his hand I told him that he was a hero in my eyes. "Why am I a hero?" he asked. I told him that I admired him because he was a veteran and he had fought for our country. He thanked me. I wanted to ask him about the war but I was hesitant because I was afraid it would bring up bad memories and he was very ill. I decided not to ask.

A week later I once again visited George and that day he seemed to be doing a little better and was quite talkative. With a little apprehension I asked him about the war and his experiences. What follows is George's story.

> Regarding the war…I wouldn't have had to go. I was working at the Princeton Mine and was told I could have gotten a deferment from CCI (a mining company) because electricians were needed in the mine. I didn't get a draft notice, but one day I went down to St. Luke's Hospital in Marquette and had a physical and a mental exam. I passed and was sworn into the army. I would leave in one week.
>
> It was February 19, 1943, and Elna, my girlfriend, and I got together early in the morning. We went to a tavern in Gwinn and danced all morning to "Life in the Finnish Woods." I had to catch a train in Marquette

at Front Street and Baraga Avenue at three o'clock. We picked up more guys in Negaunee. There were guys from Marinette, Oconto, and other U.P. towns and we had the best the nation had to offer. We were pulling a milk wagon and had to stop along the way to pick up milk. The train took us to Fort Sheridan, Illinois.

As soon as we arrived we had to form two lines. We took a test and were inducted into the army. It was an ACG test, or a military style IQ test. These scores follow you throughout the military. They found out I was Finnish and could speak, read, and write Finn. We were given military clothes and were told to ship our civilian clothes home. We were given shots in each arm, had a meal, and went to an army camp. It was named after a hot shot general from the Civil War. They sang for us, "You're in the army now, You're not behind the plow..."

We were assigned barracks, which were brand new. If you did anything wrong you had to go out in the field and clear stumps. My IQ score was high so I was made an acting corporal right off the bat.

I remember that I was only given KP duty once. I remember they hauled in hindquarters of horses. We knew the difference—they weren't cows. The older cavalry had used horses in the army and they were switching over to new mechanisms. We were there for 13 weeks.

One day a truck came by and hollered out two names. They told us to take all of our army stuff and we were being sent to North Carolina University. They programmed people there and told them where they'd go for training. We were told to go back and write a letter to our parents telling them we would be sent to where we were needed most. Later that afternoon my name was posted on a board for a language aptitude test. They wanted me to go to a school to learn Spanish. I didn't want to learn Spanish and so I signed my name and handed in a blank paper. The same thing happened later on and I handed in a blank paper. They said, "We wanted to send you to a university to study Finnish." That was the first mistake I made. I had a chance to go to one of the most prestigious schools in the United States.

I ended up being sent to Ohio University to study electrical engineering. It was an expanded program. Each term was three months long. In two years you could have a college degree. I went through the first term, which was the mechanics of physics. I was asked if I wanted to go on and I said no. So they sent me to Camp Forrest in Tennessee, where combat engineers were trained. I was assigned to the 186th Combat Engineers.

At the time I was engaged and my fiancee wanted to get married. I said no. In the army, if you get killed, you get a $10,000 insurance policy and my mother had raised me until this point in my life. I wanted her to have that. I was given a week's leave and went home. I danced and sat around and "swooned."

After my leave I was sent to Fort Jackson Carolina where we were to get ready to go overseas. We didn't know where we were going at the time. We were sent to Florida where we boarded a ship. We were on that ship for 31 days, docking in New Guinea where we stayed for two days. The ship carried mail for the GIs there, which they were very happy to receive. We were then loaded up to invade the Philippine Islands, which Japan occupied during that time.

While in the Philippines one of my comrades was hit by shrapnel that took off most of his leg. I spent most of the night guarding him. I could tell he was in a lot of pain and I went to look for a medic. There were dead bodies and wounded men lying all over the field. He was lying under a trailer that held many gallons of aviation fuel. I didn't find a medic and so I went back to be with him. Later, since he was in so much pain, I again went to look for a medic. While searching for a medic a Jap stuck his rifle butt in my abdomen. I grabbed his rifle and I was so angry that I hit him in the face with the rifle and I kept hitting him with monotonous regularity.

When we left the Philippines we landed in Japan and we were sent to Hiroshima. The United States dropped an atom bomb…and Japan surrendered.

They eventually began to ship men home, and when my time came up I went to a camp where you'd be sent back to the United States. A truck came by and stopped and I was told to get in. When I got into the truck a guy from my hometown, John from Princeton, Michigan, was in the truck! We headed to Camp Mc-Coy, Wisconsin, got discharge papers, and got on a train to Little Lake Michigan. My mother and my brother were there to meet me.

The next day I met my fiancee Elna. It was grand to be home! It was so wonderful choosing who I could go with and where I wanted to go.

When I would close my eyes at night and go to sleep, however, I would relive the war. The whole war passed before me in my dreams. Today there is a name for it. It's called PTSD.

Later, George and Elna got married and they had two children. Their first-born was a little boy. The second child, a little girl, was born on September 9, 1948, at home. George delivered her because they couldn't get to the hospital in time. It was quite an experience!

His son was later stricken with polio and went through many years of operations and therapy. He later graduated from

Michigan Technological University with a bachelor's degree in engineering.

George worked as an electrician in the iron mines until his retirement. During his retirement he had a bad accident and had a serious, closed-head injury. He had never spoken about the war very much. I had known him since I was a child and I didn't know that he was a veteran of WWII until many years later. As George was spending his last days in a veterans' facility fighting lung cancer, I visited him many times and it was at this time he related his experiences of the war to me. However, as I left the hospital that day, he teased me and said he was mad at me because after talking about the war he would have nightmares when he went to sleep that night.

During my childhood years I had spent many happy days in George's home with him and his family. As a child I would sit on the back steps of their house waiting for my friend Lynn, his daughter, to come outside and play. George was always so sweet and kind to me. My father had passed away when I was 15 years old and George and his family made me very welcome in their home. It all seemed like yesterday, those wonderful '50s and '60s, and now it was 2007. George was 85 years old now and preparing to meet his Lord. On September 9, 59 years to the day after he had delivered his baby girl at home, George passed away peacefully.

George had received an honorable discharge from the army and had received numerous awards, including the Good Conduct Medal, Meritorious Unit Award, the Asiatic-Pacific Campaign Medal with two Battle Stars, the American Campaign Medal and the Philippine Liberation Ribbon.

Arne

Arne was drafted and sworn in on November 14, 1942, in Marquette, Michigan. He entered the army on November 27. He went in with another guy from my hometown (Palmer, Michigan) and one from Gwinn (a neighboring town). He did his basic training at Fort Blanding, Florida, and felt it was no problem for him.

Arne went overseas as an MP, and traveled to Africa and back and then to the European continent and back. He was in Africa for a short time, Scotland, England, France, Holland, Belgium, Germany and then back to France. His job was to transport prisoners to New York. They traveled on big ships—ocean liners. One ship was the *Empress of Scotland*, converted into a troop ship.

> We couldn't travel with lights on at night because of the submarines. They would have torpedoed us, so we had to run dark and silent. Prisoners were housed in the bottom of the ship. They were pretty quiet. We all just sat and stared at each other.
>
> I spent a good amount of time in France. There was a tent city. There were thousands of tents and a couple million troops there waiting for an available ship to take them back to the United States.
>
> Desertion, murder and rape were all considered capital crimes. I saw an American soldier get hung. He was charged with the rape of an old woman. The prisoner was standing on a scaffold and they had to wait for the doctor to arrive before they could proceed. The doctor had gotten lost on the way and the guys in charge were getting madder by the minute. He eventually arrived and the guy was hung.

Arne was in the army four days short of three years. He said the worst part was putting in the time. He was discharged in

1945. He said when he came home he went camping, worked in the woods and later became a pipe fitter. Arne lives a simple life and a kind of isolated existence. He loves to hunt and years ago did a lot of fishing on Lake Superior. He does a lot of reading, including the Bible. When things get too noisy at his home on the lake, he heads for a hunting camp in the woods where it's quiet. Material things mean very little to him. He lives alone, enjoys nature, and does some welding to keep busy. He puts out bird feeders in his yard and loves animals. There are always lots of birds, squirrels and even the neighborhood dogs around.

Arne is 87 years old now. We asked him what he thought about the things that were going on in this country, such as in Iraq, and he said he thought our country should keep its nose out of other countries and take care of our own problems.

Arne was awarded three Bronze Stars, the American Theater Service Medal, the European African Middle Eastern Service Medal, and a Good Conduct Medal.

According to Dr. Dan Forrester, quoted earlier for his work with veterans and PTSD, the difference between the Vietnam verterans and World War II veterans was that "many of the veterans of World War II spent weeks or months with their units returning (from war) on ships from all over the world. During the long trip home, these men had the closeness and emotional support of one another to rework the especially traumatic episodes they had experienced together. The epitaph for the Vietnam veteran, however, was a solitary ride home with complete strangers and a head full of grief, conflict, confusion and joy."

Post-Traumatic Stress Disorder In the Community

"I'd like to get to the point that when I put gas in the lawn mower I think about mowing the lawn rather than pouring it on myself and lighting a match."

A veteran recovering from PTSD

The Effects of PTSD on Families

Living with a veteran is definitely a challenge at times if they have come home scarred from trauma. It is especially difficult because most wives have no idea where all the turmoil and anger come from. Until the problem is diagnosed, most wives are frustrated, and many now suffer from secondary post-traumatic stress disorder.

The following are first-hand accounts of spouses and children who have lived with a veteran suffering from PTSD.

Judy

The Vietnam "Conflict" changed meaning for me shortly after I married Jim in 1972. I did not know him before he went into the Marine Corps, so I was not aware of anything different about him. Jim did quite a bit of drinking, but once we were married, that had to change or he would not have been able to function in the workplace. I had known that he had knocked his mother across the room when she tapped him on the shoulder when he was taking a nap, and I was the victim of that same experience when I tried to wake him to answer a phone call. He came up swinging and hit the wall close to me. Moods would change and you could never predict what would set him off. He blamed people for incidents that were undeniably his fault and sometimes would stare into space or be so exhausted that he would sleep for hours.

Our first son was born three years after we married and things seemed to be going well. Both of us were working hard and we had moved into our first real home. I noticed that Jim would drink a lot around the fourth of July and parades were not something he enjoyed. I asked several times why he didn't get involved with the Vietnam group marching in the parade, and he would say that he wanted nothing to do with them. He would not talk about the war and said he wanted to forget all about it. Three years later our second son was born and the stress of everything began to take its toll. As the kids got older they tried to do things around the house and yard, but they never seemed to do it correctly. Jim would fall asleep in the living room shortly after work and stay there for hours. We started camping, and the stress of packing and getting ready would put Jim in such a state that we often did not enjoy the weekends. Road rage was common and we would be nervous wrecks hoping he didn't start a fight or force someone off the road. He didn't trust many of the people we met and would become particularly upset if people started talking about the military.

I thought about leaving many times. Trying to teach and coming home to someone whom I felt did not support me emotionally left me feeling very much alone. Jim would threaten to go "into the woods alone to think" and there were many times when I asked him to seek help. His mother had told him when he returned home from Vietnam that he had changed. Jim was sometimes a tyrant at home but so nice in public, and I found myself resenting his "nice guy" public persona. His family had no idea what life in our house was like. I often stayed home when he went to family functions just so that I would have time to unwind.

Jim was an involved father when the kids were young and coached several of their hockey and baseball teams. I give him a lot of credit for putting so much effort into helping and sometimes thought he did that so he wouldn't have time to think about what was haunting him in the horrible nightmares he regularly experienced.

Work was driving Jim over the edge. He was made a lead man responsible for a crew, and he could not understand why certain members of the crew would not do the job correctly. He took everything as a personal slap in the face and several times had problems with other employees or supervisors. He worked hard, but he knew that the lead position was wearing him down. He asked to be relieved of these duties, but supervision did not want to lose him.

About four years ago Jim came home and said he was retiring, that he could not stand it any longer. We had recently built a new home and I was not expecting news of that sort. There was no talking; his mind was made up, he was retiring. That was about the time that an old friend talked to him about PTSD. All the symptoms fit. Jim had started to talk a little about his Vietnam experiences and I felt that putting a name to what he was living was a step in the right direction. It has not been easy. Facing what happened so many years ago has opened doors that were almost closed.

Lots of tears, more nightmares, and talks with family members ensued. Medication changes create a raging monster one week and a sleeping giant the next. I face a lot of restaurant walls so that Jim can have his back to the wall. People think it's funny that he jumps a foot when someone taps him on the shoulder; I don't do that anymore. I like my teeth just the way they are. He is sometimes irrational, and I have learned to use humor to make light of the situation. The kids are supportive and are happy that he has sought help. Communication is pretty easy and we laugh about some of the earlier incidents now. They weren't funny then. Sometimes they were scary.

Jim's dad was a POW in World War II and has suffered with what is now known as post-traumatic stress disorder for years. He avoided crowds, was sometimes confrontational, and everyone tiptoed around his moods and habits. This is not something that I want passed along to my kids, and I believe that education and communication have been a positive influence. Both of my parents were in the military during WWII, and I was always proud of that. The Vietnam "Conflict" happened a long time ago, but its repercussions have changed the lives of far too many survivors and family members.

Chris

We have had to undergo lots of counseling over the years. There was lots of silence. He just didn't talk. He drank heavily for the first five years of our marriage. He worked a lot. After work he would go to AA meetings five days a week. He suffered from depression and wouldn't talk. He was suicidal. I received a call at work one day from his therapist saying that I needed to get someone to go with me and find him. When we finally found him he was walking out of the woods. His intention was to commit suicide and light a fire in the trailer. He'd thought that if he committed suicide he would have taken me out with him. He didn't want me to be left behind. He knew then that he needed help. He spent two years living in the basement, isolating, suffering from PTSD and depression. He would spend most of his time reading stuff about PTSD and veterans' stories. It took five years of counseling before he would file a claim with the veterans administration.

We attended couples' counseling groups and I attended women's groups. It seemed like we always had a lot of company because when he finally began to recover there were lots of people that we were trying to help. He spent 15 years participating in a veterans support group and another 10 years facilitating it.

This veteran's wife cried before she came to meet with me that day. She had spent so much of her life dealing with her husband's PTSD, and so much time helping other wives and talking about it, that she was finding it very difficult. However, because she felt that it may help other wives and families to read about her experiences, she came to the interview. She and her husband are reasonable happy these days and although PTSD veterans are never completely cured, it appears that they are living a normal life and have found healing.

Barb

I always liked going to parades and the fireworks around the fourth of July. Jim never seemed to want to go with me and so I usually went with my kids or a friend. But one year I didn't have anyone to go with. Jim didn't really want to go but I said, "Jim, why don't you want to go with me?' I would have had to go alone. So Jim decided he would go along. We took our lawn chairs and walked down near the harbor and watched the fireworks. I loved it and was in awe over the beautiful fireworks display. Jim just sat very quietly through the whole thing. He usually hid things very well. Afterwards I asked him why he was so quiet. He told me that the fireworks reminded him of the flares in Korea. I felt bad. I didn't know. Many wives have no idea of the triggers that bring their husbands back to trauma.

I now know that if my husband has a bad day and is not himself that there is usually a good reason for it. It may be a bad dream or the smell of diesel fuel. Now I usually try to figure it out before getting angry.

"People Wouldn't Understand"

I have been entrusted with some very personal stories. Before their husbands were diagnosed with PTSD, their lives consisted of living for years hiding dysfunctional behaviors that they dealt with on a daily basis. Here's what another wife shared with me.

> I couldn't talk to my friends about what I was living with because most people are able to cope with life and problems in a normal manner. I didn't think anyone would understand.
>
> My husband overreacts to little things and he doesn't trust anyone. At times he seems to have feelings of paranoia. He doesn't sleep at night and sleeping pills don't help. He avoids social situations and wants to spend a lot of time alone. He is helpless in most situations and I have to take care of him. I come home from work and he is sitting in front of the TV and doesn't want to be bothered. I have to fix his meals, get his clothes ready, pay the bills, and be responsible for all the decisions in the household. He explodes over nothing, whether it's looking up a phone number or dealing with a stack of mail. Everything is a crisis in life. If the phone rings the first thing he thinks is that there's a problem—trouble. If something important comes in the mail it must be trouble. He is never really happy, usually seems to be either angry or depressed. He drinks too much.
>
> We fight over it. He can't stand in long lines in stores and is rude to store clerks. He doesn't seem to care what anyone thinks.

Why Wives Stay With Their Husbands

Why did these wives stay with their husbands? Many wives left and couldn't deal with all of the turmoil in their lives. Those that stayed often thought about leaving, but knew that something was wrong and remembered the person they fell in love with. They hung on to the hope that they could find a solution. They were trying to protect and care for their husbands, but also tried to shield their children. They became exhausted, walking on eggs, always anticipating the worst behavior. They were confused because they usually knew a loving side to that person, but anger was just beneath the surface.

Holidays were a disaster most of the time. One wife says, "I'm tired. I'm so tired of the abnormality of my life. I want someone to take care of me."

Once husbands were diagnosed, most wives felt a sense of hope. They received some education about PTSD and now understood why their husbands acted the way they did. Now when things went wrong they knew what was behind the anger and bad behavior and it was easier to deal with. Knowing their husbands were learning coping mechanisms took some of the confusion out of it.

Most of their husbands were now taking medication for depression and anxiety and attending therapy groups, talking with other combat veterans. For many there was healing and hope for a better life. However, some of their husbands still suffer from addictions with drinking and gambling in addition to all of the behavioral issues. For these women, life is still difficult and they struggle from day to day. Many husbands had to hit rock bottom—losing their jobs, wives, family, and friends—before they were willing to honestly work on their problems.

Wives should have the opportunity to attend group counseling to deal with their feelings. However in most cases, neither insurance or the VA covers the costs and it is not affordable for the family. They suffer as much, if not more, than the veteran, and the VA should have some type of help that is funded for families.

This is where churches, synagogues, mosques, ministers, priests, and rabbis need to realize how important counseling services are in religious organizations. There is a great need to understand PTSD and what it does to marriages and families. Those who are unable to afford the counseling will be left out. The veterans (and others who suffer from PTSD) need understanding and support in their desire to find peace, along with the courage to go on.

PTSD in Caregivers and Families

According to sources, many partners of veterans with PTSD have a greater chance of developing mental health problems. These wives tend to assume a greater responsibility for household tasks such as finances, house upkeep, time management and maintaining relationships within the family and the extended family. Most wives are very concerned about the veteran's problems and feel compelled to take care of them. They become aware of the triggers that can set the veteran off, and they try to minimize these situations. This eventually results in a feeling of "walking on eggs" and anxiety. The symptoms of PTSD, along with avoidance and emotional numbing, interfere with the intimacy in the relationship and contributes to problems in maintaining good intimate relationships. Many of these spouses have been close to a nervous breakdown at sometime during their marriage. It is very important to these families that they receive counseling and become educated about PTSD.

Divorce

Many of the veterans I have interviewed have had relationships that failed and have been divorced several times. According to sources, approximately 38 percent of Vietnam veterans' marriages failed within six months of their return home. Divorce rates of veterans with PTSD are even higher than those returning from Vietnam without PTSD. Anger, irritability, and emotional numbing—all symptoms of PTSD—all contributed to the failure of marriages. Alcohol and drug addictions are extremely difficult to live with, and often wives felt it was a hopeless situation with no solutions.

"Please, God, Make My Daddy Happy."

The following was written by a child whose parent suffers from PTSD. Her experiences mirror those of almost any child living with a parent with PTSD.

> I wanted to cry. I hated when my dad got so mad at us…but I needed to be strong so my mom wouldn't think I was upset. It would only make her really mad at Dad if she knew I was upset, and then she might cry or yell. I hated it when her neck would get all red and the tears would swell up in her eyes and then pretty soon her voice would turn into a straining whisper. You could tell she was having a hard time breathing as she fought back the tears. She looked so stressed and upset, you could hardly hear the words that came out. Then they would fight…really fight. I just wanted everyone to be happy. That's all. Couldn't we all just be happy?
>
> My heart was racing. I wanted to throw up, and I wished I could turn down the volume of his voice. Or turn it off. He was really mad! He kept swearing and saying, "Why are these goddamn coats all over the bench every day? Learn to hang them up or I'm gonna throw them out the goddamn door! Don't you know how to pick up after yourselves? How many times do you have to be told?' Or, "Get the hell in here and get this goddamn mess straightened out! And who left their bike in the driveway? How the hell many times do I have to tell you, how am I supposed to get in the garage if your goddamn bike is in the way?"
>
> I was always taught not to use God's name in vain and my dad did it every day.
>
> The ranting didn't stop. My brother and I would run around putting the shoes and coats away. My dad would grab a beer from the refrigerator and would just

keep saying the same things over and over and was so mad. We couldn't clean up fast enough. I didn't want my mom to see how upset I was because it hurt her to see us kids unhappy. I'd swallow the huge lump in my throat and fight back the tears. I thought he must be very disappointed in me for not being a better kid. I needed to try harder next time. How did I let this happen today? I wanted him to be pleased with me. I guess I just screwed things up a lot.

He was like this, angry, every day when he came home from work. I hadn't seen him drive up, but I wish I had. I could have tried to get upstairs before he came in just in case he was in a bad mood.

Later on, after the yelling, he would come and find us. He'd tickle us or tease us to make us laugh. He knew what he had done and how harsh he had been. He knew he shouldn't have acted the way he did and frightened us when he'd yell. He was sorry. He was trying to make up with us, but he'd never admit he had over reacted or that he was sorry. I guess it was all he was capable of. It was good to see him smile and happy to see us. I'd pretend to be happy and not hurt. It was just easier that way. No one seems to care what a kid thinks anyway.

My dad always told us he loved us and he'd hug and kiss us all the time. I knew that he loved us, but I didn't know when or why he would be mad next. It was always like waiting for the other shoe to drop. Soon something would happen and he would blow up. We tried to enjoy the time when he was happy because we all knew it wouldn't last. It was like waiting for a time bomb to go off. You never knew when.

I didn't know it then but I was growing up with a father who had PTSD. However, I did know from a very young age that something was wrong with him. I think I even knew that deep down inside he really couldn't help it when he blew up and that it wasn't us he was mad at. He was just really, really unhappy and desperate to feel some kind of peace. I prayed for it all the time. "Please God, please make my dad happy." It made me so sad to see him so unhappy.

As the evening progressed, things would become more relaxed. It seemed like Dad was happier now. He was watching TV and looking at a magazine. I wanted to tell him something about school, but maybe it was best that I just leave him alone in the family room. Just then, he'd get up and come into the kitchen. He was agitated and angry. He'd been watching the news. Something had triggered that anger again. He hollered about the dog, the garbage, the president, everything or anything. My heart would race when he got upset and I would stare intently into my schoolbook. "How's my girl?" He'd lean over and kiss me on the cheek and say, "You're such a smart girl. I have the best kids in the world. I love you."

Throughout my childhood this change of moods was a part of my life. I never knew what things at home would be like at any given time. I never liked bringing my friends home because he was very unpredictable. He had even yelled at my friends on other occasions. They were all kind of afraid of him and didn't like playing at our house. I was always anxious for the day I could go out and live on my own and not have to worry about these blowouts anymore. I could love my mom and dad from a distance and not have to take this stress any longer.

There are many emotions to deal with as a child of a person who has PTSD. There is a lot of confusion, self-blame, doubt, a need to please, a desire to be positive and make everyone happy. I felt responsible for drowning out the negative, guilt, worry, anxiety, and low self-confidence. The sad thing is, I know now that my dad never meant it. He had a hard time functioning each day as a normal person. He didn't mean to hurt us. He was sick and needed help. He really did love us so much.

I love my dad so much. I always have and I always will. I am so glad that his PTSD was finally diagnosed and he got help for this problem. He is learning to work on dealing with the things that trigger his anger and set him off. But sometimes I feel cheated. I only wish he had this kind of help many years ago while I was growing up. I could have enjoyed him so much more as a child. But the good news is that I can enjoy him as an adult. I am so proud of him for dealing with this problem head on.

We have been a much happier family since he has begun going to counseling and group therapy. I thank God for answering my prayers. My dad knows he was in a very dark place and said and did things he is not proud of when we were kids. But he has always told us how much he loves us.

As an adult, I have seen how living with PTSD has affected me and my own coping skills. I have clinical depression and an obsessive-compulsive disorder. I cannot tolerate yelling or overreacting to issues. I startle easily and have drowned many of my emotions in overeating. I am lucky, though. I learned that these issues affected me at a very young age and have worked very hard to resolve them. I don't blame anyone.

As a parent, I have also learned that you are doomed to make mistakes. But if there is love—your kids know you're not perfect and love you anyway. Love is the most important gift you can give your children, and I always knew that my dad loved me...no matter how hard things got. You need to move on with your life.

I love you dad!

As indicated in the above account, the unpredictable behavior and emotions that a person suffering from PTSD exhibits leaves the family with psychological wounds. The startle response manifests itself as hostility. The person may be a fanatic when it comes to cleanliness and order and the family constantly walks on eggshells. These children are deprived of a normal childhood. There is an over protectiveness and the parent is over demanding. Children become afraid of not living up to a parent's expectations. They grow up afraid to make loud or sudden noises. They live in fear of setting off a trigger that will set the veteran off.

The person who suffers from PTSD and relies upon alcohol or drugs to medicate themselves in order to cope with life makes it harder for their families to deal with this. Frequently the family also suffers from secondary PTSD and needs to get counseling.

Childhood Abuse and Trauma Related to PTSD

People who have been exposed to childhood trauma or abuse are frequently more prone to use alcohol and tobacco excessively. Stress and trauma in childhood often leads to risk-taking behavior such as the use of drugs or mood altering substances. Also, the person who has endured childhood trauma is more susceptible to PTSD.

Pre- or perinatal trauma, which can occur in abnormal maternal/infant bonding, may also contribute to a kind of childhood trauma which can make the person more susceptible to PTSD later in life during traumatic experiences such as a war. For example, the mother of a newborn infant was extremely ill due to postpartum depression. For the first two years of the child's life, the mother was incapable of responding, or bonding, with the infant. He was cared for by relatives until the age of two when his mother recovered and resumed her role as mother. The two had a wonderful relationship from that time on and his mother showered him with love and affection. However, later, as a veteran of the Vietnam War he suffered from full-blown PTSD.

It is possible that the lack of bonding could have had an influence on him years later. One veteran, as a young man, had to deal with several suicide attempts (the last one successful) of his father. This was very traumatic for him and his family.

Trauma freezes us in past events and affects our perception of reality for the rest of our lives. That traumatic event is always in the back of our minds, ready to intrude on our daily lives and triggered by the littlest things.

The Healing Process

What can you do if you have a spouse that possibly suffers from PTSD? Some of the following things I have learned and done may be helpful for you.

Talk to your spouse and calmly explain that you think their behaviors indicate they may have a problem. Be supportive.

Contact a VA representative to get permission to get an assessment by a psychologist who works with veterans. Once you get an appointment you will be answering some questions and filling out some simple forms.

A psychologist will meet with the veteran and make an assessment. He/she will then advise you as to what you will need to do next.

It will be important for you to sit down and write an honest letter explaining what the veteran was like before he went into combat or experienced some type of trauma, and how he has changed since that time. It should be detailed and include everything that you consider to be a problem or abnormal behavior. (For example, angry outbursts, jumpiness, alcohol or drug problems, a tendency to isolate themselves, and so on.) After it has been completed enclose it in a sealed envelope and include it with the papers you will be filing for a disability claim. It is not necessary for your spouse to read it. (I didn't want to hurt my husband any more than he was hurting at the time.)

Your spouse will be receiving one to one counseling for a period of time until they are ready for group counseling. Be supportive and encourage your spouse to go to regular counseling sessions. You may go with him after the first initial appointments if he wishes. You might be able to help him open up by bringing up particular incidents, in a kind and tactful manner so that he doesn't feel like he is being attacked or criticized.

Sometimes a veteran is hesitant to go for help, or to admit needing help. One veteran was worried that his wife would leave him. He was also expecting his first grandchild and didn't want that child to know the person he was at the time. Sometimes the fact that he may receive financial help if he is struggling at work (a disability from the government) is the only incentive that will bring a veteran to ask for help.

Now that you know more about post-traumatic stress disorder you will probably be more sympathetic to the problems he had that made you frustrated and angry. You may still feel angry, but keep in mind that these behaviors are the result of stress reactions stemming from trauma. It is usually triggered by something that probably doesn't have anything to do with you. You are merely a sounding board. You are that safe person that he knows loves him and stands by him and so you are the one he will probably lash out at. These reactions stem from fear and a survival instinct directly related to his combat experience. Everything to him is a crisis situation, whether it is looking up a phone number or opening up the bills in the mail. Remember that a trigger such as the smell of diesel fuel, the sound of a helicopter going over, or just a hot humid day can send him back to the war in a second and all of the fears and feelings will come back.

Look for ways to ensure that he lives in a quiet, calm environment. Soft soothing music rather than loud boisterous music is more calming. Give him some quiet time alone. We had a comfortable family room where it felt safe and relaxed. Sometimes watching the news on television, especially the war in Iraq or Afghanistan, is not a good idea. It may trigger thoughts and feelings that are uncomfortable. In terms of diet, limit the amount of caffeine, alcohol, sugar, and white flour if possible. Try to encourage your spouse to get enough sleep and some exercise. A short walk helps to eliminate anxiety.

Your spouse may be prescribed medications such as an antidepressant or antianxiety medication for the times he is extremely agitated or angry, medication that will enable him to sleep without having nightmares or flashbacks.

Talking with other veterans is helpful especially if he is in the company of a therapist. However, constantly rehashing war experiences with other veterans without the help of a counselor may only instill more anger and anxiety. Group therapy with other veterans is very helpful.

Keep in mind that he will be uncovering feelings that have been kept buried for years. He isn't going to get better over night. It will take time. But assure him that there is hope. If you see improvement in his behavior and feel that there is some healing taking place, tell him, and encourage him.

Talking calmly and kindly about your problems and solutions is good. He needs to know also that his PTSD has affected you and your children and that recovery is important to everyone. It is difficult for a child to live in an angry, dysfunctional environment and it is necessary to do everything possible to protect them.

It is important for the whole family that this problem isn't ignored for a long period of time. Children are in the formative years and living in an environment where there is a lot of anger. Everyone constantly walking on eggs is not normal or healthy.

The veteran who is unable to ask for help eventually will spiral into a destructive situation. They may possibly self-medicate with alcohol or drugs. He may eventually turn to suicide. He needs to know that none of this is his fault, and that he is having stress reactions that stem from his time in combat. He needs to know that there is hope and he can get help. He needs reassurance that he can one day lead a peace-filled life if he will only reach out and trust his counselor.

Paperwork and Finding a VA Rep Who Can Help

Soldiers who have been suffering, unknowingly, from PTSD for years are now coming forward to receive treatment. Treatment costs are beginning to soar. Many of these veterans did not recognize that they had serious problems for years. Many thought they were going crazy and did not want to seek treatment out of fear.

The veteran who experiences extreme trauma in combat is usually the one who eventually suffers from PTSD. Records of trauma were not well kept in the military, however, so there are times when soldiers misrepresent the truth in order to get compensation. However, in most cases, assessments are accurate because there are awards given for valor and exemplary performance. Those who were not recognized for something special are required to have letters from other people who witnessed the action to verify that it did happen.

Poor documentation during the Vietnam War is a detriment to the veterans seeking claims. Not only did they have to serve, now that they need medical help they need to provide proof, many years later. Yes, there is some misrepresentation, maybe a handful, that slip through the cracks who don't deserve the compensation, but why should a legitimate case of a veteran who has gone through trauma have to look back years earlier to prove his case, all because the government did a poor job of documentation?

Many of these veterans, because they do suffer from PTSD, are unable to endure going through the paperwork process. They have a feeling of helplessness. Relying on an advocate to help them is a trust factor and the whole process is 300 to 500 days long. In addition to a lack of patience and concentration, the process becomes overwhelming to them. Furthermore, the Vietnam veterans are being pushed aside because now the Iraqi veterans need care. Where is the care the Vietnam veterans need?

To provide treatment for those who really need it, it is important that each veteran is screened. All of the veterans I have interviewed have had assessments done by a professional therapists and were then sent on to a VA hospital to be further assessed by psychiatrists. The findings are then sent on to Detroit (or depending upon which state you live in) for further study. In the end, most veterans are screened extremely well.

Vic Romback has worked as a veterans service representative with Vietnam Veterans of America for 11 years. He is a Vietnam veteran who served with the United States Air Force and is a vital piece of the puzzle in aiding veterans, especially with the paperwork. He has helped a lot of people to submit claims, get through all of the red tape, and get benefits from the veterans administration.

Many veterans come to Vic for help. Many are sent to him due to problems they are having on the job, or by wives who feel their husbands are in need of help. What percentage of disability or benefits the veteran gets from the government depends upon the severity of the veteran's problems, whether they are physical, psychological or both. According to Vic, many veterans are in denial and either won't ask for help or are brought in by other veterans who recognize the importance of the help they could receive.

It is important that you know that Vic is a veteran himself. He has more insight into the importance of helping other veterans. Let me share an example.

Several years ago a veteran from Wisconsin was unable to get any help. A severe case of post-traumatic stress disorder had him almost debilitated. When he finally got the courage to go to the Wisconsin county office for help to get information about his veteran's benefits and help, he was promptly turned away. He made a trip to the Upper Peninsula in Michigan to a veterans support group, which met at the Vietnam veteran's office in Negaunee, Michigan. There he was supported by fellow veterans and given the appropriate information to find a therapist and help in the Wisconsin area, who by coincidence was a Vietnam veteran who was very compassionate. The veteran today has received psychological help as well as financial help, which he is grateful for.

Assistance is available at any VA medical center, vet centers, or VA regional offices. The toll-free phone number for the VA regional offices is 1-800-827-1000. Also, most veteran service organizations can direct a veteran to a veterans service officer.

The Benefits of Counseling

What happened to the guy who used to laugh and joke? He used to be carefree and happy. That was the tall handsome guy with the laughing brown eyes. Where did the young man go who loved to be with his fiancee, who wanted to be with her day and night and was brimming with love and hopes and plans for the future?

He has gone away and someone else came back; someone who has pain and sadness in his soul. There's anger in him, like a stormy sea ready to erupt. His peaceful sleep is no more. He dreams horrible dreams of the past and sleeps with a gun nearby. He awakes wet from night sweats and can't see the blue sky or the sun. He doesn't notice the chirp of the robins or smell the freshness of the clean spring air. His glass is half empty all the time and he lives only to survive, waiting for a crisis, 24 hours a day.

He feels so alone and thinks no one understands him or knows how he feels. He keeps it bottled up inside, until one day his anger becomes overwhelming and he explodes like a bomb. His anger is like a railroad train with no brakes. Once it starts he can't stop it…

He is tired and sad. He's hurt the ones who love him the most and his heart is aching. "I feel like I am going crazy." No one hurts more than he does, and people are turning away.

Then one day a ray of sunshine comes through. A hand reaches out to him. The voice says, "I understand, it isn't your fault." The face is kind and he listens. "I am here to help," he says. Tears fall, the dam breaks and a flood of guilt, emotion, sadness, and worry rushes through until it turns to a trickle. A weight has been lifted from his shoulders. "I understand," the voice says. "You are not alone. There are many others like you. It isn't your fault."

Then he meets the others. Soldiers, veterans like him who are hurting and angry inside. They talk, they feel each others' pain and grief. They pick each other up and help one another. They care. They understand. Each time they meet and talk, they drink coffee and together learn to cope. The leader, the kind voice, the compassionate one, guides them to the light at the end of the tunnel. He teaches them and tells them why they are hurting and so angry. He helps them to learn to overcome their anxiety and triggers of anger. Sometimes they laugh and enjoy each others' company, but sometimes they swear and have regressed. The week had been a bad one.

But they are safe here. They can vent and be honest, and the others relate to his feelings and pick him up off of the ground

A group of Vietnam veterans get together for coffee and socialization.

once more. He brushes himself off and once more goes out into the world. He is a little wiser, a little stronger, and the future is filled with hope for a while. This feeling may not last, but now he is not alone anymore. There will still be bad days…but most days will be better.

Why Veterans Avoid Help

Even though getting help and counseling is beneficial and even life-saving at times, many veterans avoid getting help. Why is this?

Dr. Dan Forrester has a Ph.D. in social work from Columbus University, a master's in social work from Michigan State University, and is a graduate of Lake Superior State College. His comments have appeared earlier throughout this book. He is a veterans adjustment counselor at Bell Behavioral (part of Bell Memorial Hospital in Ishpeming, Michigan) and has a satellite office in Marquette, Michigan. He has been working with veterans with PTSD for the past 20 years, long before PTSD had a name. In his experience counseling veterans with PTSD,

Dr. Dan thinks they avoid treatment for a variety of reasons.

Dr. Dan Forrester

> Many veterans are hesitant to go for help first because they are not aware of the fact that there is such a thing as PTSD, and second because they are afraid to open up old wounds for fear they can't deal with it and would fall apart.
>
> Vietnam veterans have avoided treatment for the following reasons:
>
> 1. No one really wants to hear about it.
> 2. No one would understand.
> 3. "I can handle it myself."
> 4. "I'm afraid they will lock me up because I am crazy."
> 5. "I don't trust anyone."
> 6. "I'll be seen as weak."
> 7. "I don't want anyone else to find out."
>
> Consequently, many Vietnam veterans continue to address their problems much as they did in Vietnam and upon their return home. They dealt with it on their own, kept it inside, and self-medicated with alcohol or other drugs.

Here's what a few veterans have said, in their own words, about their hesitancy to go to counseling.

> I didn't want to come here. I am afraid I am weak. I am afraid I am crazy or something. I can't tell my family what is going on because they wouldn't/couldn't deal with it and I think they would think less of me.

It's very hard to come here. I haven't talked to anyone about this for 33 years. But recently my wife left me and I find myself with a loaded .45 contemplating killing myself.

I should be able to deal with things myself. It's very difficult to accept help from anyone. I have had several marriages. You wouldn't believe how tough it's been to keep a job. I should have been fired many times. I feel like I'm taking time and money away from more needy veterans by being here. There are others more deserving.

It's hard, it's very hard. I wasn't going to come here, but my wife told me I had to or she was leaving me. I should be able to handle this on my own. I guess I haven't been doing a very good job of it. I guess maybe its pride. Hey, I'm a marine, we are supposed to be able to deal with stuff.

I've just kept it in all these years. I've went about my business as best as I could. My first wife said that there was something wrong with me. And now this wife says I need help. I'm afraid to be here because I don't know what will happen if I have to talk about some stuff. There are things that I have never told anyone. Do you think I am crazy?

The Counseling Process

Each week a group of veterans get together to help one another. Their leader, Dr. Dan Forrester, has been with them since day one, educating them about PTSD and how to cope with it. It is important that the veterans know and hear that they did not deserve what they've endured and that they did not cause it. They need to know that they deserve to recover. They also need to hear that they aren't crazy, that PTSD is a normal reaction of a normal person to abnormal circumstances. People even from the most stable upbringing and environments will experience PTSD after certain combat experiences.

It is crucial that the therapist or group encourage the veteran to express his grief and emotions. Group therapy can be instrumental in providing the support the veteran needs to forgive himself.

Conventional therapy for PTSD involves years of individual or group therapy. Repeated stress wears you down both in body and mind and healing comes from a process. Finding support is a part of healing. It takes time to heal. At times patients become discouraged with therapy and drop out before they are able to resolve their problems. However, the person who remains in group therapy finds support and learns how to deal with their problems. Together the group is able to find solutions and healing.

Dr. Dan Forrester explains the goals of the counseling process:

Education is the first step in the sometimes-long process of readjustment. The soldier enters the service with noble intentions but very often encounters events more intense than they ever realized and lasting longer than they had been prepared for. There is a psychological, emotional and spiritual impact from which the veteran needs support and time to readjust. For some they may feel shaken to their very foundation as they struggle to survive and to find meaning amidst the intensity of life and death events. The very things they did to survive continue even upon their return home. What was adaptive for wartime conditions, however, becomes maladaptive within the community and family to whom they return.

It is important that the veterans come to understand that what they are experiencing is not mental illness nor is it a weakness within them. Rather, it is a stress condition, the result of traumatic intensity on the level of life and death. The task of recovery is to make the adjustment to being home, accepting that their life will be forever changed due to their experiences. But they do not have to carry the weight of continuing in a survival mode, replaying the intensive memories, feelings of guilt, sadness and anger. There can be a coming home.

I have gained much compassion and admiration for veterans of all wars as I have provided readjustment services over the last 20 years. In the 1980s the total number of suicide deaths among Vietnam veterans was between 150,000 to 200,000. There, of course, have been many more since that time. The estimate is this grows by 14,000 per year. My hope and my purpose in working with veterans is to provide them with a feeling of appreciation, hope and mutual trust so that they might receive the support they need to complete the journey home. It is on many levels that healing takes place.

What is often not discussed is the spiritual journey that many veterans must make to regain balance in their life and purpose. I have talked to many veterans who felt they lost their souls in combat. They feel that they have committed transgressions from which there is no forgiveness, nor do they feel that they would deserve it. They question if there is a God and why God would let war happen. For this, we enter into a discussion about what is the nature of God and also the nature of man. We refer to their honest intentions when they entered the service, and how it was others who made the war and determined how it was to be fought. They were trained to be the best soldiers and to fight a war for their country. What they did not know is that war itself is not fought without the unexpected and without mistakes being made. They did what they were trained to do. They did it to the best of their ability.

We look at the concept of forgiveness and why they feel that they alone cannot be forgiven. We look at guilt and purpose to gain perspective and to find balance. When at all possible, veterans are referred to treatment groups with other veterans who together can support each other to find the answers, to end isolation, to find improving social skills and the ability to communicate.

Does counseling really help?

The comments below have been shared by veterans who have been part of the counseling process.

I don't want to dwell on the past. I've tried for years to bury it and would do anything to forget. But it haunts me and I need some help. I am in counseling now, digging up what I tried to bury for years. It seems to undermine my thoughts continually.

I need to take full strength antianxiety medication as I became very angry today because of communications with our car insurance agency. It was a very bad day. I really upset my wife and I felt very, very terrible. I just can't handle a crisis anymore. Everything seems to be a big deal. I will go back to my group therapy on Monday. I can't wait because they are all so helpful. It happens to them, too.

Yesterday was my daughter's thirty-fifth birthday. I tried to call her but never was able to reach her to wish her a happy birthday. Group therapy was tough today in the end. Two of us talked about second-guessing ourselves that cost others their lives. I had a bad night. I was back in Nam, much older, but was being interrogated by commies, and took a lot of abuse for my involvement but didn't crack under pressure. I woke up exhausted. I told my wife it was the worst night I put in since I got home from Vietnam. This shit comes out in group. It has more impact than one-on-one counseling. At least I did it this time. This shit is haunting me all over again. Son of a bitch.

Today we had a full house. There was a lot of discussion of things to do or consider to bring yourself down from obsession over a problem or confrontation, anxiety attacks and the "run away train" with no brakes, because we are usually alone with no one to defuse the situation or calm us down. We need to make a checklist of things that help us.

One member of the group has gone off to a hospital for treatment. He's had a lot of addictive behaviors with alcohol and gambling. He's been at rock bottom for some time now and needs some supervised care. We all wished him well as he left today. We hope to get progress reports as we have all become very involved in his recovery effort.

I had a one-on-one therapy session with my therapist. He is always a big help to straighten out my thought process. I had a bad week and needed the extra attention.

It is my first day back from a Colorado hunting trip. I went to "Charm School" (group therapy) today and relayed my experiences and how close it was to a return trip to Nam. It had been 38 years since I had a rucksack on my back while packing a rifle with all of my supplies to live in the wild. I had to constantly remind myself that I was on a wild game hunt, not a search and destroy mission. It was very difficult the first couple of days. I deer hunt locally, so I was not prepared for this experience. I was in the central highlands in Vietnam, and the mountains in Steamboat Lake were very similar. It gave me an uncomfortable feeling of a return to survival. I later accepted the beauty of the area and decided to help others carry out their prize bulls and I didn't carry a gun on the rest of the trip. That made me feel better about being surrounded by nature, rather than hunting and using skills to ambush quarry.

I took pictures instead. I fished one day and enjoyed the surrounding beauty of the small mountains that were completely forested and very challenging for an old soldier. I got home safe with some meat and a rack 4x4 from one of the other hunters. I was glad to be home safe in my own home.

Group was all about gratitude. We had good participation and the group seems to be moving in a positive direction in developing better coping skills. Topics covered included the ability to make good choices and addiction.

The Costs of PTSD

For many reasons, the time a young person puts in serving his country in the military makes him a better person. Boys become men and they learn responsibility, self-discipline, and physical fitness. It gives him a sense of being prepared and boosts self-esteem. They find that they are able to do things they never thought that they could do. All of the veterans I spoke with were very proud to have served their country.

On the other hand, there is a tremendous cost to war. Although most people in the United States are against the war currently going on in Iraq, I believe the majority of them have no idea what the repercussions of war will be for this country. Not only will many of these men come home with emotional problems, but they will pass these problems on to their families to deal with. If by some chance they are diagnosed with PTSD, they will probably be unable to function unless they receive many hours of therapy to help them cope with everyday life.

In many cases, wives and children may also need counseling. The government will be footing the bill, and rightly so, for all of the healthcare these veterans need. Those veterans who are 100% disabled will need disability payments from the government for the remainder of their lives, which is going to cost the country dearly.

Not only will PTSD hurt our country financially, but it can cause an otherwise stable person to go off the deep end, either harming themselves or others. I have heard it said by veterans, "I get so angry with so and so that I could kill him." We have all heard in the news about the person who has walked into a place of employment, extremely upset with authority figures or coworkers, and started shooting everyone in the place, killing innocent people.

Another cost of PTSD shows up in a large portion of the homeless men in the cities who are veterans that have turned either to drugs or alcohol, probably due to undiagnosed and untreated cases of PTSD. Due to the depression, the alcohol or drug dependency, as well as an inability to go through the red tape to get the help they need, they live in the streets. There is a kind of helplessness and hopelessness in them.

According to the United States Department of Veterans Affairs, on any given night approximately 250,000 veterans are homeless in the United States. (Between 529,000 and 840,000 veterans are homeless at some time during the year and make up 23% of the homeless population.) Of these:

- About 45% suffer from mental illness.
- 47 % served in Vietnam.
- 76% have alcohol, drug or mental health problems
- 45% need help finding a job
- 37% need help finding housing
- 67% served three years or more
- 85% completed high school

Even returning veterans from the Iraq war are having trouble finding jobs and are ending up homeless. They are living on the streets, in cars, or sleeping on a friend's couch within weeks of returning home. After putting their life on the line they come back home to nothing. One veteran slept in his car or on the streets or on a friend's sofa.

Many Vietnam veterans are still homeless. Many suffer from PTSD, substance or drug abuse. They were never able to make the transition back to civilian life. It took approximately 12 years before many of the Vietnam veterans began to show up at homeless shelters. It took time for the results of the trauma they went through to surface. Even when PTSD is diagnosed in a veteran the time it takes to process the claim leaves him with no income. Between the process of being unable to function in society after the war, and the lack of jobs and finances, as well as the time it takes to process a claim (provided they are even capable of going through the process of all the assessments, paper work, doctor appointments, and possibly a need for medication due to anxiety or depression), a lot of time can go by. It is not uncommon that during this time the veteran is without a home or income. Although there is help from the veterans administration as well as veterans groups and private community agencies, some veterans are so impaired that they do not, or cannot, reach out for help.

America's homeless veterans are not limited to those who have served in Vietnam or Iraq. They include veterans from wars in WWII, Korea, Grenada, Panama, Lebanon, Afghanistan, and Iraq. In fact, the history of homelessness goes back to the Revolutionary War with the term vagabond. We've all heard about vagrancy. The term bums and tramps can be traced back to the Civil War era. These were men who rode the rails and were victims of physical and psychological damage as a result of experiences from the war.

Homelessness would have affected WW II veterans more if it weren't for the GI Bill, which aided veterans and the improvement of the United States economy during that time.

A few years after the Vietnam War a wave of homeless veterans in their twenties and thirties began to appear on the streets. Throughout history there has been a high incidence of homelessness as a result of disabilities, both physical and psychological, due to war combat.

The next time you see a homeless person on the street ask yourself, "Could that person be a veteran? Could that person be someone who fought for our country?"

Reaching the Conscience of Others

One of the reasons many veterans never learn about PTSD or receive treatment is because they have never been alerted, or diagnosed, and the government claims they can't afford to treat all of the veterans. The government spends all of its funds on the war and weapons.

The government asks so much of the veterans but can't always give much back to them. We need to reach the conscience of the government and politicians who have the ability to fund things properly to help families, putting things back together for them. There is a high cost of course. But this is only part of the high cost of war. Whom did these men fight for? What are these wars all about? Who are the young men who are called to war? Frequently it is not the affluent and the wealthy. It is often the young people who cannot afford an education who join the service. It is often the poor or middle class American families who send their sons to war.

Although life has improved significantly for our family, Ted will always have problems. If he attends his therapy group every week he can usually cope well with life, but if he misses one or two meetings the old symptoms creep back. Recently he began to talk about dying at a young age once again. He began to worry about how I will manage financially if something happens to him. He is only 59 years old. I had seen this type of thinking many times over the past years and didn't understand his fear. Now I know that it is one of the symptoms of a Vietnam veteran. Most veterans don't believe that they will live very long. My own counseling sessions had helped me recognize many of the symptoms which had once upset me, but now I was finally able to understand.

As reported in the January 2007 issue of VFW Magazine, about 176,000 veterans from the wars in Iraq and Afghanistan are looking to the VA for compensation. A New York Times article last October reported that a former VA analyst estimated some 400,000 returning GIs could eventually apply for benefits. These are staggering numbers.

It is imperative that we reach the conscience of the government and politicians who have the ability to fund things properly. We need to help families put things back together again. The body heals, but brain injuries from traumatic experiences in war require a lifelong healing process. Just because you don't see blood doesn't mean that the wounds are healed. These men fought for our country and the government needs to care. They cannot be just forgotten. Their lives and the lives of their wives and children are drastically affected by the after effects of war, which in turn greatly influences our society as a whole.

I'd like to close with the words of Dr. Dan Forrester. "Just as there has been tremendous progress in understanding PTSD over the last 20 years, we continue to stand on the threshold of even greater understanding. We must be diligent in our continuing to move ahead to make support services and treatment available to all veterans who need them. Though funding for veterans services tends to become a political issue, we must let veterans know that we support them and that they are appreciated. It is right and they are deserving that we do so."

To the Reader

I began to keep a journal during the time Ted and I were going for counseling, which eventually was the start of this book. Although I didn't particularly like the idea of opening up our lives to the world, I knew there had to be other families, not only in the area that we live in but all over the country, that dealt with the same problems and were searching for answers. By writing about our experience we were hoping to reach out to others. If this book helps one family in the healing process it will be worth it.

I did not write this book in an effort to be creative. You may not have been hanging on the edge of your chair. My main purpose in writing this book was to get the word out, to make people aware that people who experience trauma in war come back psychologically scarred. They have given their all. They have sacrificed a lot. So when you hear that someone has gone off to war, pray for them. When they come back from war, thank them. War changes people, and not always for the better.

So in reading this book, don't be judgmental of the veterans and their mistakes and behavior since they returned. They didn't start out that way. Their war experience changed them. And although they may not have been perfect before they left, they have been affected in a way that has damaged their personalities and their lives. Still, each of them is a hero, and my husband Ted and I sincerely want to help them. Someone was there to help us and now it is our turn to return the favor. By purchasing this book, you have helped them as well, and we want to thank you.

The veterans who participated in this project had many problems when they returned from war. Yet today most of them have been able to put their lives back together again. Once stuck in time, they are now able to put the war behind them for the most part, and are concentrating on making their lives better. The thoughts of suicide come less frequently, and the depression is in control, and they work on coping mechanisms. They have been educated about PTSD and recognize the triggers that set them off and send them back to the bad memories of war. They are now finding peace. Medication and counseling has helped them to lead much happier lives. And perhaps most importantly, there is once again hope.

Bibliography

Dyhouse, Tim. "One in Four Iraq and Afghanistan Veterans File Disability Claims." VFW Magazine, January, 2007.

Everstine, Diana, and Everstine, Louis. *The Trauma Response*. New York: W.W. Norton & Company, 1993.

Forrester, Dan. "Combat Related Post-Traumatic Stress Disorder: A Comparison of Vietnam and Iraq War Veterans." Ph.D. diss., Columbia University, 2007.

Goodwin, Jim. *Readjustment Problems Among Vietnam Veterans, The Etiology of Combat-Related Post-Traumatic Stress Disorders*. Cincinnati: Disabled American Veterans, 1980.

Kennedy, Robin. "Walking Wounded." Master's thesis, Northern Michigan University, 2007.

President's Commission on Mental Health. "Mental Health Problems of Vietnam Era Veterans," Vol. 3, 1978.

Price, Jennifer L., and Stevens, Susan P. "Partners of Veterans With PTSD: Caregiver Burden and Related Problems." National Center for PTSD Fact Sheet.

Riggs, D. S., Byrne, C. A., Weathers, F. W., and Litz, B. T. "The Quality of the Intimate Relationships of Male Vietnam Veterans: Problems With Post-Traumatic Stress Disorder." Journal of Traumatic Stress, November, 1998.

Scaer, Robert. *The Body Bears the Burden*. New York: Hawthorn Medical Press, 2001.

Scaer, Robert. *The Trauma Spectrum: Hidden Wounds and Human Resiliency*. New York: W. W. Norton & Company, 2005.

Schiraldi, Glenn. *The Post-Traumatic Stress Disorder Source Book*. Lincolnwood: Lowell House, 2000.

Solomon, Z., Waysman, M., Avitzur, E, and Enoch, D. "Psychiatric Symptomology Among Wives of Soldiers Following Combat Stress Reaction: The Role of the Social Network and Marital Relations." Anxiety Research, 1991.

Williams, T. *Post-Traumatic Stress Disorders: A Handbook For Clinicians*. Cincinnati: Disabled American Veterans, 1987.

Order Form

Please copy this page, add the necessary information, and mail it with your check or money order, payable to Milly Balzarini to:

Milly Balzarini
110 Oakridge Dr.
Marquette, MI 49855

ISBN: 9781930374270
The Lost Road Home $19.95 each   Qty. _____

Total: _____

MI residents add 6% sales tax ($1.20/book) _____

Shipping: $3.50 first book, $1.00 each additional _____

Total enclosed: _____

Name: _____

Address: _____

City: _____ State: _____ Zip: _____

Phone: (__) _____ Email:_____

You can also order this book from DeForest Press at www.DeForestPress.com. To order by phone, call DeForest Press at 763-428-2997, or toll-free at 1-866-509-0604.